BDS *for* IDIOTS.

BOYCOTT ISRAEL honestly –

and let's see how far you get!

Also by Barry Shaw:

Israel Reclaiming the Narrative.

Fighting Hamas, BDS and Anti-Semitism.

BDS *for* IDIOTS

BOYCOTT ISRAEL honestly –

and let's see how far you get!

Dedicated to those who prefer truth to lies and facts to fraud...

...a seriously funny humiliation of BDS.

CONTENTS

FOREWORD.

"My friend, I'll say it clear I'll state my case, of which I'm certain...

For what is a man, what has he got?

If not himself, then he has not

to say the things he truly feels,

and not the words of one who kneels."

Frank Sinatra – and now me about BDS lies.

"There may be times when we are powerless to prevent injustice, but there must never be a time when we fail to protest."

Elie Wiesel – and now me about BDS fraud and injustice.

"Who can challenge the rights of the Jews in Palestine? Good Lord, historically it is really your country."

"The idea itself is natural, fine and just. Who can challenge the rights of the Jews in Palestine? Good Lord, historically it is really your country. What a wonderful spectacle that will be when a people as resourceful as the Jews will once again be an independent nation, honored and complacent, able to make its contribution to needy humanity in the field of morals, as in the past."

Yusuf Diya al-Khalidi, the Arab mayor of Jerusalem, in 1899 in a letter to Zadok Kahn, the chief rabbi of France about the rights of Jews to self-determination in the land of the Jews.

ACKNOWLEDGEMENTS.

It's time we had a book that exposed the fraud of what is known as BDS.

BDS is not an organization that need be feared. It is an amalgam of disparate radicals who have cobbled together a cause to attack Israel.

Their hyper-active extremists have become a nuisance that attempt to get in the way of progress; progress to peace, progress to prosperity for Palestinians, progress to Israel's advanced economy.

They are ineffective economically, but they are part of the problem for lack of progress in peace talks. In effect, BDS is anti-progressive.

BDS is a three letter metaphor for negativity. In their practice, their initials stand for Bias, Deception and Slander.

We need to out them, to name them, and shame them. They need to be exposed for the intimidating fraudsters they are.

It's time to humiliate them. This book does that with facts, anecdotes and humor.

Voices heard in this book include

CAROLINE GLICK the senior Middle East fellow at the Center for Security Policy in Washington, D.C. She is also the deputy managing editor of The Jerusalem Post. She is the author of *'The Israel Solution.'*

PAT CONDELL's acerbic political commentaries found on YouTube have delighted and offended thousands. His rapier wit pierces political incorrectness leaving the viewer with a smile on the face and a nod of the head in appreciation of his well-turned phrase.

EDGAR DAVIDSON's articles came to me like a refreshing light casting the glow of humor against the malevolent misuse of words. Anything that makes the reader smile and look again at hateful language surely turns people away from the harmful influences of BDS.

ALAN DERSHOWITZ is a Harvard law professor and a leading defender of civil liberties. As such, his words carry the gravitas of an international figure renowned for his fairness and the application of justice to both sides of a cause. He is the author of the best-selling book *'The Case for Israel.'*

BASSEM EID is a Palestinian human rights leader. He is courageously outspoken not only about Palestinian rights, but also the rights of Israelis. As a Palestinian human rights activist he is vociferously against BDS and Israeli boycotts, because they end up harming Palestinians.

MATTI FRIEDMAN is a respected journalist and author. His dissection of the ideological roots of media bias against Israel is a masterpiece. His new book is *'Pumpkinflowers: A Soldier's Story.'*

HOWARD JACOBSON not only won the Man-Booker Prize for Literature with *'The Finkler Question'* in 2010, he was shortlisted for this prize again for his work *'J'* in 2014. His thoughts on the world today from his Jewish perspective makes to enlightening reading.

DENIS PRAGER is the president of Prager University and a radio host.

MITCHELL BARD is the author of the book 'The Arab Lobby.' He is also the Executive Director of the American-Israeli Cooperative Enterprise.

I thank them for their wisdom, their insight and, yes, even their humor.

IF YOU'RE GOING TO BOYCOTT ISRAEL – DO IT PROPERLY.

Guidebook for BDS Idiots.

Dear BDS campaigner and Israel boycotter,

OK. I know you have an issue with Israel and are in love with the Palestinians.

That's OK too, but I understand that, because of this, you want to boycott Israel.

As an Israeli I'll be sorry to miss you but, if you're going to boycott my country, do it properly.

It's easy to tell people to picket stores that stock Israeli products, trash their shelves, and insult the customers, but don't you think you should set a personal example?

Don't you think it's wrong for you to be telling others to stop using Israeli items when you yourself are using them? Isn't that a little bit hypocritical?

So, together, let's see what you are using and make sure you really being true to your cause.

I had thought of sending you this letter by email but that would have compromised your principles. After all, most Windows operating systems were developed by Microsoft-Israel. The Pentium chip technology that gave birth to Microsoft's success and the global spread of computers was designed by Intel in Israel and the Centrium processor was entirely designed, developed, and produced in Israel. Isn't that a pity!

Voice technology was developed in Israel. The technology for AOL's instant messaging was developed by four young Israeli whiz kids. So I guess that cuts out you're messaging to your supporters and to those you want to boycott us.

All of Africa is connected to the internet and Facebook thanks to the Israeli Amos 6 satellite. So that reduces your chances of recruiting people on that continent.

You can't even store stuff. Your DiscOnKey was developed by Israel's M-Systems. Your firewall technology came from Check Point based in Haifa.

So, sorry! To be true to your cause, you have to throw away your computer.

But your bad news doesn't stop there. Get rid of your smart phone. Even if it is made in Japan or China, it's got an Israeli brain!

Not only did Microsoft and Cisco build their only facility outside of the United States in Israel. IBM, Qualcomm, Autodesk, Oracle, all have substantial R & D presence in my country. Even Apple has opened its first non-USA R & D center in Israel.

Google bought Waze, the Israeli navigation system, for a billion dollars. Texas Instruments developed their Bluetooth chip at their Kfar Saba laboratories, and that's in Israel. Motorola keeps on investing in Israel because it makes perfect sense in developing new innovations brought to their happy customers by Israeli scientists and technicians.

So now you have to throw away your smartphone, because you can't have anything to do with Israel. That makes you kind of dumb, doesn't it? But, hey, that's your boycott principle, right? Don't try to sell your now useless stuff on eBay. Forget it! Their shopping technology comes from…. Yes, you got it! Israel. It's also Israeli technology that operates the PayPal payment system.

You'll find that life is difficult when you can't tap into your electronic information and that instant communication that made your life more efficient. You'll find yourself isolated from the world you knew when deprived of the technology that was brought to you by Israel.

So now you are computerless and don't have access to a smartphone. What a shame! You'll miss all the other Israeli innovations that made using your phone so much fun.

I want you to know that while you are incommunicado, Israel is keeping you safe. Israel's strategic cooperation with your country, your city, and your banking system in combating cyber warfare that is also preventing your national grid from crashing, that keeps your municipal transportation system operating safely and your financial systems from enemy hackers.

This is where Israel's advanced technological expertise is helping to keep citizens in your country safe from the threat of global terror. This may upset you, but it's true.

Feeling insecure? Feeling your health breaking down? Sorry to hear that but, before you reach for your pills, stop right there! All generic brands fighting heartburn stem from Israeli laboratories. In fact, check the labels of all your medication. Make sure you don't have anything marked from Teva and Abic. These Israeli pharmaceutical companies are world leaders in prescription drugs.

It will probably mean you will begin to suffer from colds, flu and worse but, hey, that's a small price to pay for your personal crusade against Israel, isn't it?

While we're on the subject of your Israeli boycott and our medical contributions to the wider world brought by Israeli scientists, researchers, chemists and doctors, how about telling your friends to avoid the following;

An Israeli company developed a simple blood test that can differentiate between mild and more severe cases of multiple sclerosis. So, if you know anyone suffering from MS, tell then to swerve this Israeli patent that may, more accurately, diagnose their symptoms. To be honest though, I think they'll ignore you.

An Israeli-made devise helps restore the use of paralyzed hands. This devise electrically stimulates the hand muscles giving hope to millions of stroke sufferers and victims of spinal injuries, some caused by terror attacks caused by the people you support. If you wish to remove this hope of a better quality of life from these people, go ahead and tell them to boycott Israel.

By the way, Israeli inventor, Amit Goffer, invented the ReWalk that enables paraplegics like him and Israeli Arab, Radi Kaiof, to get out of a wheelchair and do something they never thought they would ever do again – walk! But I doubt that they will listen to you. Certainly the American Veterans Administration isn't. They have just agreed to pay for the Israeli-invented robotic legs for paralyzed veterans. People want to see soldiers, sailors, airmen and Marines stand up after becoming paralyzed fighting for their country. This is what ReWalk does. It restores pride and self-confidence to heroes like Marine Captain Derek Herrera. He was paralyzed by a sniper's bullet in Afghanistan in 2012. Now, he has a new life thanks to ReWalk. *"It's a game-changer for me. It changed my mindset. It makes me hopeful for the future."*

Tell me, would you remove this man's future because of your hatred of Israel?

I'm sure you know that boycotts affect scientific research. I guess you don't really care about that.   But a research center in Israel, the

Neuroscience Center in the Sheba Medical Center at Tel HaShomer Hospital is trying to throw light on brain disorders like depression (I guess you are starting to feel depressed right now) and Alzheimer's disease. So which do you prefer? To have your depression deepen, or have it cured by Israeli medicine and medical advances?

A new molecular-level imaging technology from Israel can detect diseases in cells. It can also target cancer cells directly without harming healthy cells. Aposense is a rare company that is fighting against cell deaths for the good of mankind, but particularly for cancer sufferers. But I guess this doesn't move you.

Israel's Hadassah Hospital has successfully eliminated the physical manifestations of Parkinson's disease in a select group of patients by the application of a deep brain stimulation technique.

An Israeli arthritis treatment has been found to reduce high blood pressure. There has also been a recent Israeli research breakthrough in insulin-producing cells for diabetics.

A new medical device, the Exblate 2000 System, uses a guided ultrasound beam to target and destroy uterus fibroids and non-cancerous masses found in the uterus. It's developed by InSightec in the north of Israel and has been approved by the US Food and Drugs Administration. It's a life-saver for many women.

Hot off the press! As I am writing this, news just came in that Israeli scientists at Ben-Gurion University announced a breakthrough in HIV research. This is going to leave you with a terrible dilemma. Try telling your gay friends to boycott this future product.

The team said that their findings will result in a *"revolutionary diagnosis and the key to the clinical solution to prevent the HIV infection and it will destroy the deadly virus."* Boycott that!

Are you really going to head a campaign to persuade people to boycott the Israeli genius that saves so many people's lives and improves the quality of life for so many more?

Are you really that mean-spirited?

We haven't got to how Israel is making the desert bloom; aiding underdeveloped parts of the world grow more and better crops even in the harshest of conditions. Nor have we mentioned how Israeli green energy innovation is leading to a greener planet and an improved ecology.

These are just the tip of an amazing Israeli Start-Up nation. Think of the enormous contribution Israel has made that benefits people all over this world, including the Palestinians you claim to help. I will put our contribution next to yours, any day.

Pro rata of population, we are making a greater contribution than any other nation on earth. If truth be told, we really aren't as bad as you make us out to be.

What is bad is your BDS campaigning. What is deceitful are people like you, who promote boycotts of Israel. The initials BDS stand for *'boycotts, divestments and sanctions.'* To we Israelis, you stand for bias, deception, and slander.

Your campaigns have not been effective. Economically, for Israel they are not even a pin-prick. While you have been campaigning, the Israeli economy has grown tremendously. The world loves our quality products and, in many cases, can't live without them.

There's a joke going round, and it's at your expense. A few people may join your protests and propaganda against Israeli products. But, without the noise you make outside stores and supermarkets that carry our stuff, a lot of people wouldn't have known where to buy them. Thanks for bringing public attention to where they can buy our great stuff!

The sinister truth is that people like you are not campaigning for a *'two-state solution'* but for a no-state solution, a world without Israel. Your appeal for human rights stops dead in its tracks when it comes to Israeli rights.

So, be a person of principle. Stick to your hateful boycott cause. You've thrown away all your Israeli-based hi-tech and genius, you are unable to spread your cause without them, you are sick and getting sicker with boycotting Israeli medication and science, and as you lie at home (because the hospital and surgeons in the operating theater will be using Israel imaging and technology) feeling bad, allow me a final word.

The wonderful innovation and creativity that Israel offers the world with love will beat your message of hate and negativity any day!

This is a reworking of an article I wrote about nine years ago that went viral on the social media.

There is an open-minded, fair, public that sees sense. There are also people who have been drawn into misguidedly supporting a malevolent, emotion-driven, false narrative that subjects Israel to a slander that is not applied against the most evil regimes on the planet.

This book is addressed to these misguided souls and malevolent haters.

Sadly, there is more need for this book today than there was in the days of my original article.

The Jewish philosopher, Moses Maimonides, wrote the extraordinary *'A Guide for the Perplexed'* centuries ago. This book of mine could have been entitled *'A Guide for the Misguided.'*   Enjoy – and learn.

Hey, pro-Palestinian activist!

What *"human rights"* are you fighting for when you march with your *"Free Palestine! Boycott Israel!"* banner?

We all know that an independent Palestinian state would be Anti-Gay, Anti-Christian, Anti-Feminist, Anti-Western, Anti-Democratic. And not a single Jew would live there.

So, it's not really about human rights.

It's really about hating Israel.

COUNTERING BDS NEGATIVITY WITH ISRAELI POSITIVITY.
It takes a network to defeat a network.

BDS prides itself on creating a network of activists employed in a joint effort to reduce Israel's economic impact. They boast how they intend to bring Israel to its knees economically. Fat chance!

Israel's response to isolation and delegitimization has been integration and investments.

One Jewish billionaire, Paul Singer, has invested $20 million in creating Start-Up Nation Central as an integral part of Israel, the Start-Up nation.

The 2009 best-selling book *"Start-Up Nation: The Story of Israel's Economic Miracle"* has sold millions of copies and has been translated into thirty languages. As a result, heads of states, fund-managers, venture capitalists, leading hi-tech innovators beat a path to Israel to discover what makes this tiny country the world's leading science and technology genius.

More Israeli companies are listed on NASDAQ than any other non-American country.

The goal of Start-Up Nation Central is to function like a ministry of foreign affairs for the hi-tech industry in Israel and to attract investors.

On October 6, 2015, Paul Kandel was appointed to head this non-profit organization which connects government leaders and international businesses with the Israeli innovators and technologies that will help them solve their most pressing challenges. Kandel's lead team is made up of some of the most brilliant young minds that Israel has to offer.

"Among the most promising economic trends in Israel is its innovation economy," said Kandel. *"As Head of Israel's National Economic Council, I was fortunate to witness first-hand the remarkable impact that technology and entrepreneurs are having on Israel. Start-Up Nation Central exists to help enhance this trend and to bring businesses, investors, and governments to Israel – to work closely with Israeli innovators – to solve complex business and technology problems facing the world."*

Start–Up Nation Central has developed a database of five thousand Israeli start-ups across a variety of industries. It has connected over two hundred global leaders to Israel's innovation ecosystem, which helps to bolster foreign investment and trade across all five continents.

IBM, Intel, Microsoft, Google, Facebook, Apple, Hewlett-Packard, are only a few of the more than a hundred top American companies have opened R&D operations in Israel and many more have acquired companies there, bringing Israel hundreds of billions of dollars in foreign direct investment, creating many thousands of high-skilled jobs, and serving as a key catalyst for Israel's own innovation boom.

What makes Israel so advanced in innovation? It's the sense of daring linked to the sheer necessity brought about by a nation's need for survival. As Dan Senor and Saul Singer, the author of the book explain; *"Making innovation happen is a collaborative process on many levels, from the team, to the company, to the country, to the world. While many countries have mastered the process at the level of large companies, few have done so at the riskiest and most dynamic level of the process, the innovation-based start-up."*

They admit the special role that military recruitment and training plays in grooming Israel's future entrepreneurs. The Israel Defense Force's 8200 unit began as an intelligence unit specializing in code decryptions. It developed into electronic surveillance against the enemy, and finding technological solutions to IDF's battlefield problems. Its soldiers have to come up with solutions in real time emergency conditions.

The importance of this special unit is summed up by Israel's Minister of Defense, Moshe Ya'alon. *"I know Unit 8200 from my time as head of Military Intelligence and know the massive extent which their efforts play in Israel's security. The soldiers and officers there are doing God's work, night and day. 8200 preserves Israel's existence."*

It is hardly surprising that the pressure-cooker atmosphere of Unit 8200 and the talent of its soldiers, who develop critical start-up skills and experience as an integral part of their army service, translates into successful Israeli technology companies such as CheckPoint, Imperva, Nice, Gilat, Waze, Wix, Cyber Ark and Radware that all have their roots in this IDF unit.

I have witnessed Chinese leaders in mathematics, appreciative of the Einstein factor of Israel, come to find out how this little country is so advanced in mathematics and science. They have been shocked to discover a free-thinking attitude in the classroom that conflicts with their regimental methods of teaching. Thinking out of the box is a strong Israeli-Jewish trait born out of the necessity of survival.

Israel's policy of selective immigration has rewarded Israel with more engineers and scientists per capita than any other country. Jewish newcomers are granted residency, citizenship, and benefits. This immigration policy is also responsible for a meeting of minds in the dynamic melting pot of the Jewish state.

It takes a network to defeat a network. This is only one story about how Israel's economy is burgeoning. You can't boycott Israeli ingenuity.

BDS – THEIR INTENTIONS IN THEIR OWN WORDS.

Who are the leading members of the BDS campaign?

Omar Barghouti. Founder of the BDS Movement. Graduate of Tel Aviv University, a university he wants others to boycott;

"Israel was Palestine, and there is no reason why it should not be renamed Palestine."

"Palestinians have a right to resistance by any means, including armed resistance. Jews aren't indigenous just because you say you are. Jews are not a People."

When Omar Barghouti says, *"definitely, most definitely, we oppose a Jewish state in any part of Palestine. No Palestinian, rational Palestinian, not a sell-out Palestinian, will ever accept a Jewish state,"* he is not only a self-avowed racist and anti-Semite, he shows his BDS Movement to be nothing more than a puppet of Hamas and Islamic jihad whose aims he shares.

Listen to Senior Hamas official Izzat al-Risheq, publicly heaping praise on BDS advocates and activists admitting that the ultimate goal of the BDS campaign was to destroy Israel; *"We call for escalating the campaign to isolate the occupation and end the existence of its usurper entity."*

Ronnie Kasrils. South African Communist and self-hating Jew. Leading member of BDS-South Africa, that invited a convicted Palestinian terrorist to help them fund-raise;

"BDS represents three words that will help bring about the defeat of Zionist Israel and victory for Palestine."

Ahmed Mor. BDS leader and writer;

"Ending the occupation doesn't mean anything if it doesn't mean upending the Jewish state itself...BDS does mean the end of the Jewish state."

John Spritzler, BDS ideologue;

"I think the BDS movement will gain strength from forthrightly explaining why Israel has no right to exist."

As'ad Abu Khalil, Professor of political science, anarchist and BDS leader in California.

"The real aim of BDS is to bring down the State of Israel."

Ali Abunimah, BDS activist;

"The goal of BDS is the full restoration of Palestinian rights, not an agreement to create an artificial mini-state in order to save Zionism."

Norman Finkelstein, former BDS guru;

"They don't want Israel. They think they are being very clever; they call it their three tier. 'We want the end of occupation, the right of return, and we want equal rights for Arabs in Israel.' And they think they are clever because they know the result of implementing all three is what, what is result? You know and I know what the result is.

There's no Israel!"

PALESTINE – A NATION BORN IN SELF-DENIAL.

"There's no such thing as Palestine!" – A short history of Palestinian denial, in their own words.

"There is no such country as Palestine. Palestine in the term the Zionists invented. Palestine is alien to us. Our land was for hundreds of years a part of Syria." – Arab leader, Auni Bey Abdul Hadi, addressing the United Nations Peel Commission, 1937.

"Its common knowledge there's no such thing as Palestine in history." – Philip Hitti, Princeton Arab professor of Middle East history to the Anglo-Arab Committee of Inquiry, 1946.

"Such a creature as Palestine does not exist at all." Ahmed Shukari, the founder of the PLO at the podium of the UN, 1956.

"The question of borders doesn't interest us. Palestine is nothing but a drop in an enormous ocean. Our nation is the Arabic nation. The PLO is fighting Israel in the name of Pan-Arabism. What you call Jordan is nothing more than Palestine." – Yasser Arafat to Italian journalist, Arianna Palazzi, 1970.

"The Palestinian people do not exist. The creation of a Palestinian state is only a means for continuing our struggle against the State of Israel." - Zahir Muhsein, executive member of the PLO, to the Dutch newspaper *Trouw,* 1977.

"I think there is an Arab nation. I do not think there is a Palestinian nation. I think it's a colonialist invention... When were there any Palestinians? ...until the 19th century Palestine was the south of greater Syria." – Azmi Bishara, 1994.

"The truth is that Palestine is no more real than never-never land." Arab-American journalist, Joseph Farah.

"Why is it that on June 4, 1967, I was a Jordanian and, overnight, I became a Palestinian? We considered ourselves as Jordanian until the Jews returned to Jerusalem. Then, all of a sudden, we were Palestinian." Walid Shoebat, a former PLO terrorist.

"There is no such thing as a Palestinian people. There is no Palestinian entity." Hafez al-Assad, President of Syria, 1971-2000.

"Abu Mazen [Mahmoud Abbas] set off another bomb. In a television interview, he requested that the Arab states grant citizenship certificates to the Palestinians living within their borders." – Haaretz, August 21, 2005.

"Palestine is Jordan and Jordan is Palestine; there is one people and one land, with one history and one and the same fate." - Prince Hassan, brother of King Hussein, addressing the Jordanian National Assembly, 2 February 1970.

"Jordan is not just another Arab state with regard to Palestine, but rather, Jordan is Palestine and Palestine is Jordan in terms of territory, national identity, sufferings, hopes and aspirations." - Jordanian Minister of Agriculture, 24 September 1980.

"I think we have an invented Palestinian people who are in fact Arabs, and who were historically part of the Arab community." – Newt Gingrich, 2011.

A PALESTINE QUIZ.

Here's a fun quiz for 'Palestine' experts, BDS advocates and, yes, for Saeb Erekat who claims he is descended from the Canaanites.

Try answering these simple questions on your long history and culture we hear so much about as you deny Jewish history and heritage. Ready? Here goes:

When was the country of 'Palestine' founded, and by whom?

Where was its capital?

What were its borders?

Name one 'Palestinian' leader before Arafat?

What was the unique language of this 'Palestine'?

What was the prevalent religion of this 'Palestine'?

What was the name of its currency?

What form of government did it have?

Since there is no 'Palestine' today, what caused its demise, and when did this occur?

Why didn't the 'Palestinians' create a state in 1948 when invading Jordanian, Egyptian and Syrian armies captured territory in a combined war of aggression against the nascent State of Israel?

Wow! You scored really low. Could that be because there never was a state of Palestine?

A BDS PC DICTIONARY.

A compendium of politically incorrect definitions that the BDS idiots constantly apply to Israel.

Aggression: Killing people who are trying to kill you.

Apartheid: The political/social system of the one and only country in the Middle East that integrates Jews, Bedouins, Arabs, whites, blacks, Muslims, Ethiopians, Russians, Christians, Greek Orthodox, Russian Orthodox, Bahia, et al, into its state.

Arab Humiliation: The pervasive feeling on the Arab street generated by their failure to annihilate Israel and the Jews in several wars. Many opinion-makers, Middle East experts, and op-ed writers argue that Arab humiliation is at the root of the Middle East conflict; i.e., *"If only the Jews would let themselves be destroyed, the Arab street would feel better about themselves. Then there would be peace."*

Arab Spring: Replacement of one dictatorship with another, with the help of Western money and media cheerleading.

Compromise: To receive something palpable, such as land, in return for a promise not to keep on trying to annihilate you.

Developing Country: A country that is not developing.

Disproportionate Response: Winning.

Disproportionate use of force: Any Israeli military response to 8000 rockets fired into Israeli civilian areas.

Hamas: The democratically elected government of Gaza whose founding charter calls for genocide against Jews and the destruction of Israel.

Hate Speech: Free speech that progressives don't like.

Hezbollah: The democratic group whose purpose is saving Lebanon from Israeli aggression, and who's founding charter calls for genocide against Israel and Jews. The Shiite version of Hamas.

Holocaust: The genocide that did not happen, but which the Jews orchestrated it in order to steal Arab land, in which case the Jewish presence can be described as a Holocaust against the Arabs.

Honor Killings: The cultural imperative to murder one's daughter/sister/niece for humiliating male members of the family or tribe. (see "Shariah" below)

Human Rights: Only to be discussed if the subject is Arab, Muslim and preferably a Palestinian and cannot be applied to Israelis, save for pointing an accusing finger at Israel. Others may not apply unless, of course, a case can be made that Israel perpetrated crimes against them (see "Human Rights crime" below).

Human Rights crime: The credo by which murder committed by a person from a country or regime which used to be called *"Third World"* (now considered racist terminology) or a Palestinian terror group is justified (see "Resistance" below); and the defensive killing by a Jew or state, such as Israel, is bad (see "Aggression" above).

Human Shields: Integral part of Hamas & Hezbollah military strategy.

Israel: Occupied territory (see "Zionist Entity" below).

Israeli Prime Minister: Hawkish, right-winger, hard-liner.

Jerusalem: City holy to Islam in which the Jews have no history.

Jew: The source of all decadence and evil in the world; descendent of apes and pigs.

Jihad: The inner spiritual struggle for self-purification or the bloody military struggle for world domination depending on which journalist and in what language one is speaking.

Judeo-Christian Values: The credo of that civilization which has lost all its values, except that racism is bad, and diversity is good.

Koran: The Islamic Bible and radical guidebook for all the crackpot Islamic terror groups that liberal lefties says does not represent Islam when Islamic terrorists quote this book when slaughtering millions around the globe.

Leftist: Supporter of PLO (see "PLO" below), Hamas (see "Hamas" above) and Muslim Brotherhood (see "Muslim Brotherhood" below).
Mahdi: The Shia Messiah who has been hiding for centuries at the bottom of a well.

Martyr: Someone who kills someone else while killing himself. Said to be rewarded for his martyrdom by the acquisition of 72 virgins upon his arrival in Paradise, at least according to what the Prophet Muhammed (Peace Be Upon Him) said the Angel Gabriel told him (see "Koran" above).

Freedom-fighter, Militant, Shahid, Martyr: terrorist.

Moderate Palestinian Leader: Former KGB operative, Holocaust denier, and financier of Munich Olympic massacre and inciter of genocide against Jews –as long as those Jews are Israeli.

Mosque: A place for the storage of rockets and weapons to be used against Israel.

Muslim Brotherhood: A mostly secular and non-violent political party in Egypt.

Occupation: Jewish presence in disputed territory. (See "Israel" above.)

Peace: War of attrition.

Peace Process: The dismantling of Israel.

Peace Talks: The avoidance of peace.

PLO: Organization created in 1964 to end the 1967 occupation of land occupied by Jordan since 1948.

Palestinian Authority: The world's most successful kleptocracy.

Palestinian Hero: Murderer of children.

Protocols of the Elders of Zion: The authentic Jewish playbook for world domination.

Racist: An expression used by BDS activists to describe any Israeli Jew.

Radical Islamic Movement: A group whose stated official goal is genocide (see "Hamas" and "Hezbollah" above).

Recognition: A truce - until the next time it can be broken.

Refugee: Someone who has refused to take refuge, or who has not been allowed to take refuge.

Religion of Peace: The civilization with which the Judeo-Christian civilization is locked in a war to the death.

Resistance: Randomly targeting and killing Jewish civilians, particularly children.

Palestinian Right of Return: Demand to live in Israel by people who have never lived there, who hate it and wish to destroy it.

Settlement: An illegal community made up of settlers. (See "Settler" below.)

Settler: Someone who builds his house in order to thwart any chance at making peace between Jews and Palestinians.

Shariah: The Islamic system of jurisprudence which codifies and dignifies rape, child marriage, specific classes of murder such as honor killings (see "Honor Killings" above), etc.

Shia: People who are certain that Sunnis are not real Moslems, and are in fact infidels, and should therefore be slaughtered.

Sunni: People who are certain that Shia are not real Moslems, and are in fact infidels, and should therefore be slaughtered.

UNWRA: A self-perpetuating United Nations organization to promote and extend the number of refugees so as to keep thousands of otherwise unemployed UN workers in life-time careers. This is an exclusive club. Only Palestinian refugees may apply.

War Crime: Retaliation and defense.

War on Terror: Pretense that the enemy of the West is made up of small, shadowy groups motivated by childhood poverty (see "Al-Qaeda" above).

Zionism: The ideology of the Jews who aspire to control, dominate and take over the world.

Zionist: Someone who is worse than a Nazi.

Zionist Entity: The place that does not exist, as on Arab maps, but which must be destroyed.

IT'S ISRAEL'S FAULT – NO MATTER HOW BIG THE LIE.

Have you noticed how irritating the anti-Israel slogans of the hate-mongering BDS mob are? It's irritating because they are so annoyingly untrue. And yet, so many people are taken in by their lies. It's amazing, and so disappointing.

Equally irritating is how divorced the Israeli government has been over this rising tide of falsehoods leading to overseas public support.

Too many of us Israel-based advocates find the salaried officials in government ministries so uncaring in helping us with our outreach to the brave people who are standing up to the assaults against Israel being carried out at all levels of society in Western countries.

Ask your Israeli embassy if they have records of the pro-Israel activists who speak out and take to the streets in defense of Israel. I do, as do many of my Israeli-based colleagues. I guarantee that these embassies do not keep records. Simply put, they are not in the business of supporting pro-Israel campaigners.

That's why you and I fill the void left vacant by retreating government officials who constantly moan about lack of budget preventing them from representing Israel as they should. True, a bigger budget could achieve much more, but I doubt that those who have a bureaucratic chair to sit on have a clue on how to mount an effective global grass-roots campaign to save Israel from the tsunami of hate that has taken over the campuses, the media, , the churches, the trades unions and the political echelon at local and increasingly at national level in so many countries. The anti-Israel activism is widespread. It leaks into all aspects of daily life, and the official response from Israel has been - well, there isn't any! It's appalling.

It's appalling that the official voice of Israel has been missing.

The Israeli government has been derelict in their duty to defend Israel from outrageous demonization and delegitimization, in short, the slander and lies that has caught the imagination of opinion and decision makers that has caught Israel off-balance. It shouldn't have. They have been warned about what was coming for years by those of us fighting lonely battles in the war against our country.

TWO WAYS TO BE FOOLED, OR FOOLISH.

There are two ways to be fooled, or be a fool. One is to believe what isn't true. The other is to refuse to believe what is true.

Europe is guilty on both counts.

European governments employ hundreds of NGOs, NGOs supposed to foster civil and human rights for a better future in the Middle East. They fund them to a tune of hundreds of millions of Euros each year, money extracted from their taxpayers that is used to foment conflict, not peace.

These NGOs justify their existence by fermenting or supporting acts of confrontation and frequent violence in the guise of ending the *"illegal occupation."*

They produce reams of slander and half-truths against the Jewish state which is eagerly received by their European paymasters who then report to their parliaments and to the various United Nations and European Union forums that transform their documents into official condemnation of Israel.

The accumulation of unbalanced opinion pieces, posed as official reports, create a grotesque blanket image of Israel as a nation breaking all reasonable behavior, repeatedly breaching international law, ignoring resolutions,, blocking the path to peace.

Nothing can be further from the truth.

Israeli-based NGO Monitor attempts, as its title suggests, to monitor these European-funded NGOs. They have exposed many cases of NGO-published false reports and acts of provocation that go beyond the brief to which they receive their funding. They produce unsubstantiated

Palestinian falsehoods as evidence of Israeli crimes and abuse that have been taken up by the funding government. So many cases have come to the fore that you wonder if there isn't a deliberate intent by Europe to position Israel in a bad light. In these reports, the Palestinians are always the victim, rarely the villain, leaving them unblemished and Israel in a tarnished spotlight.

Further evidence of this came in the anecdotal descriptions given in Tuvia Tenenbom's excellent book *"Catch the Jew."*

Tenenbom, guised as a German journalist, ingratiated himself into Palestinian society, joined European NGOs in action in the territories, and rode in International Red Cross ambulances to United Nations camps. He reported the actions he witnessed as a guest of the Palestinians and their European collaborators. He registered the words spoken at all levels that had little to do with peace or a two-state solution. As a guest, he participated in the manufactured *"facts on the ground"* as Palestinians, aided by their willing volunteer visitors, provoked Israeli security forces into incidents that were reported as *"Israeli aggression."*

European NGOs *"educate"* Palestinian activists in how to provoke incidents designed to portray Israel in the worst possible light. Their reports, that go unquestioned in European capitals, have damaged Israel. This was the original intent. But European governments and their sponsored, trouble-making, NGOs remain unapologetic. In fact, European countries have increasingly been behaving in a more directly provocative manner themselves.

I am staggered when European governments that profess to champion human dignity act in the most disdainful manner when it comes to anything Israeli. So despicable have certain examples been that they more than smell of mindless anti-Semitism in their duplicity and double-standards.

Take the case of the Dutch government, a government with a horrendous history of behavior to their Jewish citizens during the Nazi period.

In May 2015, they decided to cut the pension of a 90 year old Jewish Holocaust survivor who left Holland to spend her final days with her children and grandchildren in the Israeli town of Modi'in. Their decision to cut this elderly lady's pension was based on Modi'in allegedly being over what is ridiculously called *"the Green Line,"* the location of the ceasefire lines between Israel and the invading Jordanian forces at the end of the 1967 aggressive war launched by several Arab armies against the Jewish state. Anyone who has visited Israel and Modi'in can have no hesitation of saying this modern Israeli town is an integral part of Israel.

The Dutch government act was one of unfeeling stupidity. So vehemently were they in their political blindness that they forgot their appalling history by punishing and victimizing a Jewish grandmother as they lashed out at the Jewish state.

As I pointed out in a June visit to Holland, during which I spoke to Jewish and Christian audiences, had she survived Auschwitz, that grandmother could have been Anne Frank. The lady in this case deserved the dignity and respect that was not afforded Anne.

So horrendous was the Dutch political position to impose such an egregious act on an elderly Holocaust sufferer that they sunk to a disgraceful low of immorality.

This move matches other anti-Israel positions taken by European governments in a procession of despicable UN resolutions.

In a session on the abuses of children's rights in warzones only one country was singled out for condemnation. Israel. By a vote of 104 to 4 Israel was isolated and pilloried. The four countries that opposed the motion were the United States, Canada, Australia, and Israel. Where were the European countries in this and other obscene anti-Israel resolutions? They were nowhere to be seen, not on this vote and not on many other fraudulent resolutions. Not one European nation stood up to oppose such false accusations in the United Nations. Not one!

Democracies have a special responsibility to teach non-democratic regimes by example the essence of what democracy stands for. Essential elements are values such as honesty, fairness, morality and truth. Not any more. Western democracies, particularly European democracies, have abandoned their principles for cynical politics. Democratic diplomacy must be muscular, not wimpy. If Western governments claim to be friends of Israel, the only liberal democracy in the region, let them prove it by opposing malevolently fatuous resolutions that are filed against Israel

Criticize Israel if you must, but oppose the blatant bias of hate and slander against Israel in international diplomatic forums.

BDS: EMOTIONALLY ELOQUENT. INTELLECTUALLY DUMB.
My encounter with a typical BDS bonehead.

It's all too easy to shoot down the rapid looneys that never sleep in their fevered hate of Israel. It's easy because they talk such cant, such rubbish. I have caught them out easily whenever I have had the opportunity to confront them, publicly and privately.

One such example was when I found myself confronted by one of the Netherlands leading BDS activists at a speech I made at the Liberal Jewish Center in Amsterdam.

He had earlier joined a meeting in the building to protest about the positive cooperation that has been going on for years between the cities of Amsterdam and Tel Aviv/Jaffa. Two representatives from the Tel Aviv Municipality had come to Amsterdam to speak with the audience about the benefits of this partnership for the citizens of the Dutch and Israeli cities. When it came to question time this BDS bonehead got to his feet to ask one of the Israeli representatives, *"Why do you train your pilots to kill children?"*

The sheer numbskull notion behind such a stupid question shows how BDS activists may be emotionally eloquent, but they are intellectually dumb.

The exchange we had was an interesting illustration of the intellectual bankruptcy of these people.

I was there for a launch of my book *Fighting Hamas, BDS and Anti-Semitism* which details the Jew-hatred at the core of the Palestinian movement, from Gaza and Ramallah through to street level activism in Europe and elsewhere. The Dutch BDS nut came to my event replete with stickers stuck to his brown shirt. (Brown-shirt? Now what does that remind me of?) His stickers displayed a Palestinian flag with the slogan 'Boycott Israel' splattered over it.

This BDS idiot claimed he had no animosity toward Jews. It was just Israel he hated.

He readily exposed the basic truth that BDS does not stand for peace, or even a two-state solution. He had no qualms in admitting that he is campaigning for a One State Solution. I reminded him that there are many many people in Israel who agree with his solution, but not in the formula that he promotes.

I warned him *"Beware of what you wish for. You may get it."* I explained to him that it's simply not possible, in a one-state solution, to have two governments.

"So, one of them has to go," I told him, *"and, as I am sure you believe in democracy, you can't have a One State solution with two government administrations and, as the Jewish population would still be the majority in such a 'one-state' world, the Knesset would remain in Jerusalem, the capital of this one-state wonder, as the administrative headquarters of this one-state. Therefore, the Palestinian Authority would be dismantled. If Mahmoud Abbas would like to stay on,"* I told him, *"he could stay on as mayor of Ramallah, no problem!"*

"But what would you do with the Palestinians? This BDS bonehead thought he could catch me out with his phony apartheid state sloganeering. I told him,

"First of all, there wouldn't be anyone calling himself a Palestinian as there would be no such country in a one-state solution. That country would remain Israel. And, yes, any citizen, Jew or Arab, who decides to be

a law-abiding citizen of Israel will certainly be able to vote as 20% of our population do today."

"What about those Palestinians who don't want to be Israeli?" he challenged me.

My answer, *"What happens in your country if you decide you don't want to be Dutch? I'm sure you have laws on this issue. I'm sure you want people to behave properly and legally in your one-state Holland, surely? If this is the way you conduct your democracy, Israel will do the same."*

I was not necessarily advocating this or any other solution to the problem. It was merely to make a point that Israel is being falsely portrayed and attacked by people like this bonehead whose argument and cause is so threadbare.

Then, in front of the audience, I told him that I would prove the anti-Semitism that he denies.

"I can prove that you hate Israel far more than you love Palestinian Arabs. You spend your live obsessed with slandering my country. You protest wherever you can wave a Palestinian flag against Israel. You tell lies about the Israeli blockade of Gaza. You fail, to tell your audience that Israel has sent it to Gaza over 1,100,000 tons of construction material at no small risk to ourselves because you know that Hamas uses this material to build terror tunnels and the infrastructure of their terror campaign against Israel, instead of using it to build schools and hospitals.

In 2012, during the earlier Hamas rocket war against Israel, we were sending between 250-280 trucks a day into Gaza, this despite the daily pounding we were receiving from them on our civilian centers. Today, guess how many trucks roll into Gaza from Israel. We now send in 800 trucks a day. Thousands of Palestinians come into Israel for medical care, including the families of the Hamas leadership. Some blockade!

Now let's look at Egypt. Nothing goes into Gaza from Egypt. Nothing! Egypt has destroyed one thousand seven hundred Hamas smuggling tunnels. Their Rafah border crossing with Gaza remains closed.

So I ask you, when was the last time you BDS people demonstrated outside the Egyptian embassy here in Holland about their blockade of Gaza? Not once? But I thought you are a concerned Palestinian activist.

How about Jordan? Do you know that Jordan has kept over a million Arabs who claim to be Palestinian in refugee camps since 1948? They refuse to give them citizenship, even though they were born in Jordan. Not only that, these Palestinians are deprived of higher education opportunities and are not allowed to work in many professions in Jordan. How's that for an apartheid state? How many times have you demonstrated outside the Jordanian embassy for their apartheid policies against the Palestinian population in their country? Not once. Why aren't you wearing stickers saying 'Boycott Jordan'?

And Syria? What of Syria? The Assad regime has repeatedly bombed and killed Palestinian residents in Syria. Why haven't you protested at the Syrian embassy? Don't you care for the Palestinians?

Why haven't you devoted your energies against Egypt, Jordan, Syria, and other Arab countries that abuse and kill the Palestinians you profess to support? Against those countries you do nothing, you are silent. Why? Could it be that you don't have a Jew to target? In truth, you hate the Jewish state more than you love Palestinians. The facts and your actions prove it. And for that, you are a Jew hating anti-Semite."

The audience sat in awe and silence. I had heard that Dutch Jews are living in fear due to the intimidating BDS-incited anti-Israel atmosphere that BDS had engendered in Holland. They are frightened to speak up publicly. I told them that they must not allow these brown-shirted hypocrites to dominate the narrative with their lies.

I told them to become fighting Jews instead of frightened Jews.

This BDS bonehead used this expression on Twitter to tweet that *"Barry Shaw had come to Holland to spread the message of hate."* I hadn't, and I addressed this BDS bonehead directly on his Twitter account.

"This was not a message of hate. It was a message of utter contempt I feel for you and your BDS lies."

On campuses, the BDS campaigners employ mob tactics. They bring in numbers to intimidate counter argument and to close down debate by overpowering anyone given a platform to present a common sense narrative in support of Israel. But, when you get them on a one-to-one basis, you quickly find them to be so shallow and emotionally-biased with false imagery that they have to resort to personal insults before retreating in anger when confronted by the bankruptcy of their argument.

As it says in the Jewish holy book, *The Mishna*, the world must stand on three legs. These legs are peace, justice and truth. Those that demand justice for Palestinians not only deny justice for Israel, but they omit the element of truth, the facts of history, the evidentiary case of Israel's legitimacy that are absent from their one-sided argument. The third leg, the one of truth, has gone missing from their monologue. A table can stand on three legs. A table built on two legs must fall. No gravitational pull can keep it standing.

Without truth their arguments are based on phony emotion but lack intellectual depth.

IT'S DOUBLE DUTCH TO ME.

While I was on a speaking and book promotion tour of the Netherlands in the summer of 2015, the Dutch Foreign Minister, Bert Koenders, was on an official visit to Israel.

During his visit, Koenders instructed his embassy to find a way to express the close relations between his country and the Jewish State. He also voiced his country's opposition to BDS.

While cultural exchanges would be a good start, a more affirmative Dutch action against the massive diplomatic injustice being caused to Israel in international forums would be far more valuable than an occasional exchange of artists or diplomats.

Much of this damage is caused by a total lack of morality by European officials, including the Dutch government.

Let me explain.

During my public speeches, I listed egregious cases of cynical Dutch diplomatic decisions that reflect badly on their government.

I mentioned earlier the Dutch government decision to cut the pension of a 90 year old Holocaust survivor who left Holland to spend her last days with her children and grandchildren in Israel. The reason given for this pension cut was that this lady's family lived over the Green Line and not, according to Koenders' government, in Israel proper. In actual fact, the family lives in the Israeli town of Modi'in which lies between Tel Aviv and Jerusalem. Modi'in was the city of the Maccabees, mentioned in our retelling of Chanukah where Jews battled the Greeks and won back the Jewish Temple in Jerusalem.

In the talk I gave in the Anne Frank Hall of the Jewish Liberal Center in Amsterdam, I pointed out that, had she survived, that lady could have been Anne Frank. This was a disgracefully act from a Dutch government with an appalling record toward its wartime Jews. That it would continue to punish a Dutch Holocaust survivor over its grievance or difference of opinion, with the Israeli government is shameful. Victimizing a 90 year old Jewish woman is no way for any liberal democracy to behave.

The shame goes on.

In my talks, I mentioned a United Nations resolution on children in warzones. The subject matter was raised as a UN motion for the sole object of targeting Israel. With a horrendous 104 nations voting Israel the worst violator of children's rights, only four countries voted against this obscene motion and in defense of Israel. They were the United States, Canada, Australia and Israel.

Notice the total lack of European nations.

Not one European country had the decency, the honesty, and the commitment to say that this motion was plain wrong. Not one European nation had the morality to vote against that motion, including a Dutch government that so often projects itself as the high moral authority when it comes to Israel.

This pattern was repeated when the World Health Organization named Israel as the worst violator of health rights. Again, no European nation had the courage to object to such a heinous charge. Holland, like all the other cynical European nations, chose to abstain rather than stand for truth and justice.

Just before I left for my speaking engagements in Holland, the Dutch government issued a travel advisory warning their citizens visiting Israel to avoid rock-throwing Jews! They get these lies from Dutch-government funded NGOs dressed up as 'human rights' groups who provide them with false testimonies and fail to report genuine crimes of Palestinian rock throwing that result in many deaths and injuries to targeted Israeli Jews.

I brought with me a Jerusalem Post news item, dated June 26, 2015, in which four Palestinians were convicted for throwing rocks that almost led to the death of Ziona Kala. Kala was in a coma for weeks following this attack on her as she was driving her car. She was luckier than most, and I listed the names of Israeli Jews who have been killed by rock-throwing Arabs. Yet the Dutch government does not issue travel advisories warning of rock throwing Arabs. That would not be political correct.

As I told my audiences, if the Dutch government does not have the decency to stand for truth and justice and, instead, participates in the ongoing slander against the Jewish State, then shame on them, and shame on all Dutch people that permit their government to continue committing such an affront against my country. I urged them to lobby their political representatives over such injustices.

The Dutch Foreign Minister said his country is opposed to BDS, but its actions aid the aims of the BDS campaign, namely the demonization and delegitimization of Israel, by their weak-kneed and cynical stance in international chambers and their own actions.

Facts and truths must be employed by the Dutch government, indeed every European government, when it comes to standing with or against Israel. They should seriously question and examine the grounds on which their anti-Israel claims are based.

Sadly, each and every European government in recent years has been swayed by cynical self-interest or ignorance by leaving Israel isolated on issues and resolutions that merit their commitment and support.

The poet, W.B.Yeats, wrote, "The best lack all conviction, while the worst are full of passionate intensity."

In the halls of international diplomacy, this is true. The worst regimes overwhelmingly pass hateful anti-Israel resolutions without objections from what ought to be decent and moral governments.

The time had come for the European diplomatic community to counter each anti-Israel motion with the truth and justice they deserve, and vote accordingly. Only then will we see the chambers of the United Nations, the EU, and the World Health Organization, being led by so-called strong liberal democracies, and not by Third World tyrants.

THE MATISYAHU SYNDROME.

While researching for my book *Fighting Hamas, BDS and Anti-Semitism* I came across a disturbing new strain of anti-Semitism.

When you see a Jew being victimized for not disassociated him or herself from Israel, you know its anti-Semitism.

Anyone who witnessed the massive global displays of Jew-hatred that rose to the surface and accompanied the 2014 Hamas rocket and missile war against Israeli civilian targets was shocked by the expressions of Jewish hate, including physical assaults and murder.

In the book I recorded instances of not so subtle forms of Jew targeting, particularly in Europe whose intent is to drive a wedge between the local Jew and Israel, the Jewish state.

In medieval days, in Spain and Portugal, Jews had to denounce Judaism and accept Christ or be punished, banished, or killed for their stubbornness if they failed to comply. Today, the aim is to force the Jew to deny his or her Zionism and accept Palestine or face punishment or death. It's as sharp a distinction as that.

One example of this modern-day form of anti-Semitism took place in 2012, at the time of an earlier Hamas rocket bombardment against Israeli civilians that brought crowds on to the streets of Europe shouting *"We are Hamas."*

It took place in the Swedish town of Malmo when Jews and pro-Israel campaigners applied for permission to hold a rally in support of Israel. They received a warning from the Socialist mayor, Ilmar Reepalu, that Jews should be careful which side of the issue they stood, for their own safety.

Earlier than that, in late 2010, the Simon Wiesenthal Center issued a travel advisory against visiting Malmo, saying, *"A contributing factor to this decision has been the outrageous remarks of Malmo mayor, Ilmar Reepalu, who blames the Jewish community for failing to denounce Israel."*

Israel's supporters, mainly the Jews of Malmo, were warned by the town's mayor that rallying for the Jewish state could be dangerous for their health. On the other hand, rallying against Israel would be, according to the mayor, acceptable.

That's why, for the purpose of the book, I called this new strain of anti-Semitism *'The Malmo Syndrome,'* a fevered urge to divide the Jew from the Jewish state by people who refuse to see themselves as Jew-haters.

It's instructive to study what has transpired in the third largest town in Sweden in recent years under this intimidating atmosphere.

In 1970, Malmo had more than 20,000 Jews. Today, there are fewer than 500. They had twenty three children in the Jewish kindergarten in Malmo. Today, there are only five left, and they have an armed guard.

The rabbi, Shneur Kesselman, is constantly abused and attacked in the streets. There have been two hundred anti-Semitic incidents in ten years.

It is no stretch of the imagination to assume that within the next ten years the Malmo synagogue will become a museum, or a mosque.

This is what BDS-type intimidation does to small Jewish communities. It changes the local landscape. I leave you to decide if this improves the remaining society, or not.

This is what Malmo teaches the Jews of Europe, and *the Malmo Syndrome* can be felt in the poisoned atmosphere of anti-Israelism that isolates and targets local Jews as it spreads its noxious fumes throughout Europe.

In a suburb of London, a coffee shop named Café Crema carried a sign that read, *"Please boycott Israeli goods. Thank you."* Later, they changed the sign to, *"We don't use any Israeli products. We are not anti-Semitic, but anti-fascist. Jews are as welcome here as anyone else."*

To the owner of this establishment, Israel was not only bad, it was fascist. Places like this pose a quandary for me, an Israeli Jew. Which part of me is allowed into the café? Am I allowed in as a Jew, or must I remain outside because I am an Israeli and, therefore, hated by him for being a fascist?

It would have made no difference, according to my Jewish sensitivity, had he hung a sign saying, *"Jewish dog owners are fascist. We love animals so the dog is welcome. The owner must wait outside."* It still comes down to anti-Semitism. In this case the anti-Semite used Israelis as the target for his barely disguised hate campaign.

Such incidents of Jew targeting are becoming increasing common in Europe. The most prominent took place in August 2015 when the Valencia organizers of the *Sunsplash Reggae Festival* decided to disinvite American-Jewish rap and reggae star, Matisyahu, from their event because he refused to sign a declaration supporting a Palestinian state. No other artists had been asked to sign such a form.

It was eerily significant that in Spain we heard echoes of the Expulsion and Inquisition of Jews calling to us from the 15th Century. Once again, a Jew was called upon to denounce his Zionism and was expelled for not doing so. In this case, the Inquisitioners were the BDS campaigners.

The global storm of protest took the organizers by surprise. Even the Spanish print media, not noted for their avid support of Israel, took up the cudgels against the organizers, calling their action anti-Semitic. It certainly was anti-Semitic intimidation that fit well into my catalogue of new-style Jew-bating.

The organizers climbed down, deciding to reinvite the artist. The highlight of Matisyahu's performance was his rendering of his song "*Jerusalem.*"

"In the ancient days, we will return with no delay

Picking up the bounty and the spoils on our way

We've been traveling from state to state

And they don't understand what they say

3,000 years with no place to be

And they want me to give up my milk and honey

Don't you see, it's not about the land or the sea

Not the country but the dwelling of his majesty

Rebuild the temple and the crown of glory

Years gone by, about sixty

Burn in the oven in this century

And the gas tried to choke, but it couldn't choke me

I will not lie down, I will not fall asleep

They come overseas; yes they're trying to be free

Erase the demons out of our memory

Change your name and your identity

Afraid of the truth and our dark history

Why is everybody always chasing we

Cut off the roots of your family tree

Don't you know that's not the way to be

Caught up in these ways,

And the worlds gone craze

Don't you know it's just a phase

Case of the Simon says

If I forget the truth then my words won't penetrate

Babylon burning in the place, can't see through the haze

Chop down all of them dirty ways,

That's the price that you pay for selling lies to the youth

No way, not ok, oh no way, not ok, hey

Aint no one gonna break my stride

Aint no one gonna pull me down

Oh no, I got to keep on moving

Stay alive"

As he took to the stage, Matisyahu was met with catcalls and shouts of *"Out! Out!"* from wavers of Palestinian flags. They shouted anti-Israel taunts at this Jewish American artist.

"These people were bullies and were trying to mess with me," Matisyahu said.

"It's fashionable to attack Israel. Some people just want to be bullies and mess with someone and Israel is a convenient target. And there's so much ignorance. Calling Israel an apartheid state? They don't have a clue to

what the situation really is. People are so quick to form opinions without investigating things on their own. And ultimately, there is real anti-Semitism that exists in the world."

By the time he finished, hundreds of people clapped and cheered his performance and his courage.

After the event, Matisyahu said that he felt he was the victim of anti-Semitism as, indeed, he was. He was sure of what he had experienced. *"To me there's no doubt. Maybe not everyone involved in that organization, but there's definitely an anti-Semitism that's there."*

For the words of his song linked indelibly to his Valencia experience, and for Matisyahu's stand for his truth that brought a global response, I have changed the name of this new strain of BDS anti-Semitism that seeks to divide the Jew from the Jewish state in honor of a reggae singer.

It is now known as *"The Matisyahu Syndrome"* because BDS and the music festival organizers tried to turn Matisyahu into a victim, but he stood tall and resisted the poisonous and deceitful hatred.

BDS LIES when it calls Israel an apartheid state.

As Israeli President, Reuven Rivlin, said on December 10, 2015, during a visit to Washington to meet President Obama at the White House, *"Israel is a confederation of minorities."*

Where, throughout the Middle East, do you find such a variety of people, religions, and cultures in one country other than in the country of Israel?

Jews, Arabs, Christians, all have freedom of speech, religion, civil rights. The Bahais have their World Center in Haifa. Druze and Bedouin are among the best and most gallant fighter in the IDF. We have Ethiopians, Yemenites, Tunisians, Moroccans, Iraqis, Egyptians and Iranians. There are Georgians, Bukharis and Circassians. We have Christian Arabs who prefer to call themselves Arameans.

Israel is a nation where a Christian Arab judge sentenced a Jewish President to jail on criminal charges. On the one hand, this is nothing to be proud of. On the other, it is indeed a country with a sense of pride in its justice system and its enabling of minorities to the most powerful and influential positions in the land.

Civil rights include the right to vote and, as twenty percent of Israelis are Arab, they have a healthy representation in Israel's Knesset. Healthy, that is, until we see Knesset members siding with enemies of the state in violent-inducing provocations. Yet, amazingly, they keep their immunity and remain in the Knesset proving that Israel is one of the most dynamic democracies in the world.

HOW MUCH DO YOU REALLY KNOW ABOUT THE ARAB-ISRAELI CONFLICT?

Take this quiz and find out.

1. When did the Jewish People establish their nationhood in the Land of Israel?

   A) In 1948, with Israel's Declaration of Independence.

   B) In 1917 after the Balfour Declaration.

   C) The 14th Century BCE, two thousand years before the rise of Islam.

   D) After the binding of Isaac in Biblical times.

2. Who controlled the 'West Bank' from 1948-1967?

   A) Palestine.

   B) Israel.

   C) Jordan.

   D) Syria.

   E) Egypt.

3. Where does the term 'Palestine' come from?

   A) The ancient tribal name of the indigenous Arab population of the region?

   B) The ancient Greek goddess that visited the Holy Land?

   C) The Romans applied the term 'Palaestina' to Judea to minimize Jewish identification with the land of Israel.

4. Before the establishment of the State of Israel, who governed the Holy Land?

    A) The British Empire.

    B)   The Arab League.

    C) The Palestinian Authority.

    D) Syria.

    E) The Ottoman Empire.

5. How many times is Jerusalem mentioned in the Koran?

    A)   700.

    B)   0.

    C)   50.

    D)   133.

6. Where do the Jewish people traditionally face when they pray?

    A)   Mecca.

    B)   The Temple Mount in Jerusalem.

    C)   Rome.

7. Haj Amin el-Husseini, the father of Arab nationalism, supported who in World War Two?

    A)   The Allies?

    B)   The Soviet advance to defeat the Nazis?

C)   The Japanese conquest of the Pacific islands?

D)   Adolph Hitler's 'Final Solution' to wipe out the Jews?

8.   About how many Jewish refugees were forced to flee Arab lands after the creation of the State of Israel?

   A)   120,000.

   B)   500,000.

   C)   6 million.

   D)   850,000.

9.   How many Arab armies attacked Israel the day after it declared its independence?

   A)   2 supported by the rest of the Arab world.

   B)   3 supported by the rest of the Arab world.

   C)   6 supported by the rest of the Arab world.

10. Who was the last sovereign power to rule the Land of Israel before the State of Israel was established in 1948?

   A)   The Palestinian Authority.

   B)   The British Empire.

   C) The Ottoman Empire.

   D)   The Davidic dynastic of the Jewish People.

ANSWERS:

Question 1. C. The Jewish People established their nationhood in the Land of Israel two thousand years before the rise of Islam.

Question 2. C. Jordan occupied the 'West Bank' for nineteen years making no attempt to establish a 'Palestinian' state despite illegally occupying the area after launching an aggressive war against Israel.

Question 3. C. There was never a state or nation known as Palestine.

Question 4. A. By virtue of the League of Nations Mandate for Palestine specifying it to become the National Home for the Jewish People.

Question 5. B. Jerusalem is not mentioned once in the Koran.

Question 6. B. Where ever they are on earth, Jews face Jerusalem to pray. Muslims face Mecca. Even in Jerusalem, Muslims turn their backs to the Temple Mount when they pray.

Question 7. D. He plotted with Hitler to annihilate all the Jews of the Middle East.

Question 8. D. The number of Jews fleeing Arab nations was almost double the number of Arabs leaving Israel. The Jewish refugees travelled further to a tiny land speaking a different language to their Arabic tongue. Unlike Arab refugees in Arab lands, there are no Jewish refugees in Israel.

Question 9. C.

Question 10. D. There has never been a non-Jewish sovereign state in the Land of Israel. Today's Israel is the third Jewish state to exist in this geographic area. All other empires that ruled the Holy Land before the re-establishment of the State of Israel were foreign occupiers who sought to colonize the area.

IS BDS EFFECTIVE IN PUNISHING ISRAEL ECONOMICALLY?

ISRAEL – AHEAD OF THE FIELD.

Israel has a unique competitive edge. That advantage is strongly based on being ahead of the field.

Historically, when other countries have caught up to the Jewish state with their products, Israel's pioneering spirit takes this tiny nation into new pastures.

Jaffa was a name synonymous with Israel's excellent oranges. It used to be a prime export for Israel until other countries captured the orange market with their cheaper fruit. So Israel turned his hand and head into experimenting, out of sheer necessity, how to battle against the harsh elements of its hot arid climate to produce food for its growing population.

This spirit of essential adventurism gave birth to fish farming, a world renowned drip-feed irrigation system and discovering how, against all odds, Israeli cows produce more milk than in traditional milk-producing countries.

This unique knowledge was patented and offered to other countries. Along the way, Israel made friends and influenced people by lending its experts to impoverished countries in Africa and Asia, helping them to become self-sufficient and able to produce crops where crops never grew before. Today, Israel runs thirty Agricultural Technology centers in India, training farmers in the latest agricultural technology and farming techniques.

This driving force of turning disadvantages into advanced thinking found an outlet in Israel's academia. For a founding nation, fighting for its very existence, putting so much emphasis into its academic research is extraordinary, but the Weitzman Institute, the Hebrew University and Hadassah Hospital were established many years before Palestine Jews earned the right to call themselves Israel.

Its genius emerged from the scientific and medical research laboratories. Under the emergency pressure of urgently finding answers to critical needs of survival, its technologists and engineers solved problems in the military field that found use in civilian and commercial solutions and developments.

Today, everyone knows Israel as The Start-Up Nation. It is fair to say that Israel was the pioneer of The Internet of Things. It led the field into a world where nobody can do without Israel and everyone in our modern world carries a bit of Israel around with them.

Not a complacent nation, Israel is already developing the technology of the future, the products that you will be using not only next year but in ten years' time and beyond.

Venture capitalists flock to Israel, eager to find bright young minds. This is a trend that BDS cannot prevent.

In sunny Israel it's raining unicorns. Tech start-ups in 2016 were valued at over a billion dollars. Israel's tech scene is going crazy.

Until 2015, brilliant Israelis looked to an exit strategy. New ideas sold to the highest bidder. When Google bought Waze for a billion dollars in 2013 it was a Eureka moment. Israeli nerds had parted with their brainchild for hundreds of millions of dollars before then but breaking the billion barrier was a watershed for Israel. Instead of selling their ideas to overseas companies Israeli entrepreneurs turned to keeping their ideas and incubators in-house and retain control of their developing businesses at home. An added benefit of this business model was that it stopped the brain drain that had seen Israel lose some of its best and brightest to Silicon Valley and other places. Israel is already seeing many great hi-tech minds returning home as the future of an Israeli-based technology industry looks brighter.

Increasingly, Israeli start-up founders are saying they have no interest in selling their successful companies. They prefer to keep their young families in Israel and grow their Israeli-based companies beyond a billion dollar milestone.

NASDAQ spotters have seen Israeli companies IPO as a new crop of public tech companies look for capital. Mobileye, Wix, CyberArk are worth over a billion dollars and others are on their way to join them.

Asian investment loves Israeli minds. Chinese money is looking to partner with Israel. Baidu, Alibaba and Tencent are just three of the major Chinese companies now tied to the Israeli tech industry. Famous Chinese billionaire and angel investor, Li Ka Shing, and his Horizon Ventures fund have successfully invested in over thirty Israeli start-ups. China has also invested over $500 million in direct investment in Israel. This is expected to double in 2016.

Rakuten, the eBay of Japan, acquired Israeli messaging app Viber for almost a billion dollars. Korea's Samsung ventures made eight serious investments in Israel during 2015. There are now Israeli companies listed on the Singapore exchange. India plans to build an R&D center in Israel. India is still restricted by its socialist legacy of bloated bureaucracy and tight regulations that stifle its economy and entrepreneurial spirit. It has a lot to learn from Israel and is willing to do so. Indian multinational companies have invested many millions in Israeli start-up and innovation ecosystems.

Over three thousand investors made their way to Jerusalem at the end of January 2016 for the 'Our Crowd' Investor Summit. They included Japanese Honda looking for Israel to develop their smart car apps.

Beat that BDS!

I shared a panel at the Global Conference on Anti-Semitism organized in Jerusalem by the Israeli Ministry of Foreign Affairs with Mitchell Bard, who was the Chairman of this workshop. I am pleased to include Mitch's take on the failure of the BDS campaign to impact Israel's international relations and economy. His fact-filled report shows the impotence of a global boycott campaign of decades that has cost them more than it has hurt Israel. As a footnote, there are clear indicators that BDS, which claims to have the best interests of Palestinians at heart, is in fact impacting badly and hurting individual Palestinian and the Palestinian economy.

THE BDS MOVEMENT'S FAILURE TO DERAIL ISRAEL'S INTERNATIONAL RELATIONS OR ECONOMY. *Mitchell Bard.*

The press is full of dire warnings that Israel is isolated and growing more so, and that the boycott, divestment, sanctions (BDS) movement is having a devastating impact on the Israeli economy. It's no mystery that Israel is politically at loggerheads with much of the world over the disastrous Iran deal, settlements and inaction on the peace process; nevertheless, diplomatic ties remain intact. Moreover, despite the desperate hopes of the BDS campaign, economic ties are flourishing.

Overall, Israeli exports have grown from around $5 million in 1948, to more than $47 billion in 2014. Israel's largest single trade partner remains the United States, despite political tensions between the political leaders. The total volume of trade in 2014 was $36 billion. In addition, each of the 50 states benefit from their ties with Israel. In 2014 alone, 21 states exported more than $100 million worth of goods to Israel, led by New York with exports of more than $5 billion.

Israel's relations are even more strained with the European Union and yet trade with the EU exceeds that of the U.S. Roughly one-third of Israel's imports and exports are a result of trade with the EU. Moreover, total trade with the EU has grown from approximately $21 billion in 2003 to $34 billion in 2013. Countries outside of the EU, the EFTA-bloc countries such as Denmark, Sweden, and Norway, have taken, or seriously considered economic sanctions against Israel. Still, Israel enjoys a free trade agreement with EFTA-bloc countries and business with these nations remains robust.

The central hub of the BDS movement is in England, but the various votes by academic and trade associations for boycotts have had virtually no tangible impact. In fact, total bilateral trade amounted to a record $6 billion in 2014, an increase of more than 7 per cent from the previous year.

The biggest economic story is the exponential expansion of Israel's trade with Asia, which will overtake the U.S. as Israel's second biggest export destination this year. China is already Israel's third-largest trading partner; in fact, since formally establishing diplomatic relations with China in 1992, trade has increased 220-fold from $50 million in 1992 to $11 billion in 2014. In addition, total trade between Israel and Japan reached $2.3 billion in 2014.

Israel's relations with India have been steadily improving, as evidenced by the planned 2015 visit of Narendra Modi to Israel, which will make him the first Indian prime minister to go to Israel. Since the establishment of diplomatic relations between India and Israel in 1992, bilateral trade and economic relations have grown from $200 million in 1992 to $6 billion in 2013. Between Modi's election in May 2014 and November 2014, Israel exported $662 million worth of Israeli weapons and defense items to India. This export number is greater than the total Israeli exports to India during the previous three years combined.

Israel is also expanding ties with Latin America and has been granted observer status in the Pacific Alliance, an economic trade organization of several major Latin and Central American countries. One country that Israel has had testy relations with because of the bombing of the Israeli embassy in 1992, and the government's failure to bring the perpetrators to justice, is Argentina. Still, economic relations are growing as evidenced by the Argentine army's $111 million contract with Israel in 2015 to upgrade 74 tanks made in Argentina.

Israel's discovery of a large reserve of natural gas off its Mediterranean coast has also opened new opportunities for expanding trade with its neighbors. Jordan, for example, signed a $15 billion deal for Israeli natural gas, and a $1.2 billion agreement was struck with Egypt. A good example of how politics does not always interfere with economics is the ongoing trade relationship between Israel and Turkey. While once close, ties between Ankara and Jerusalem grew strained as Turkish President Erdogan became more stridently critical of Israel. Nevertheless, the free trade agreement between the two countries is still in effect, and trade with Turkey hit a record of more than $5 billion in 2014, a 50 percent increase over 2009.

One of the countries hostile toward Israel that nevertheless engages in trade is Malaysia. The trade is largely one-sided, almost entirely Israeli exports, but the overall value of trade exceeds $1.5 billion, nearly double what it was as recently as 2012. Similarly, although the amount is relatively trivial, the fact that the value of Israel's trade with Indonesia is as much as $250 million is another reflection of business trumping politics.

In addition to trade, foreign investment in Israel has grown rapidly despite a brief downturn in 2014. More than 10,000 U.S. companies do business in or with Israel, including all the major high-tech companies. Intel, for example, which already has a large presence in Israel, invested $6 billion in its plant in Kiryat Gat.

Americans and other foreign investors do not invest in Israel because they are Zionists; they do it because it is a great place to do business with a creative and highly skilled pool of talent. Consider just a few of the deals concluded by American companies:

Warren Buffet invested $6 billion to buy Iscar – his first major acquisition outside the U.S. Cisco paid $5 billion for software developer NDS. Pratt & Whitney spent several hundred million dollars to buy Blades, one of the world's largest producers of machine blades. Google paid $1 billion for the Waze mapping company. IBM bought Trusteer, a fraud prevention company for approximately $800 million.

Facebook paid $200 million for a startup called Onavo. Between 2003 and 2012, 772 Israeli startups were acquired for $41.6 billion. Furthermore, despite boycott threats, Israelis are not hiding their identification with Israel. According to Economy Ministry figures, 760 Israeli manufacturers labeled their products marketed abroad as *"Made in Israel"* in 2013; that number increased to 1,024 in 2014.

Kristin Lindow, senior vice president at Moody's Investors Service and Moody's lead analyst for Israel, told Forbes in February that *"the impact of BDS is more psychological than real so far and has had no discernible impact on Israeli trade or the broader economy."* In fact, Moody's chief economist, Dr Mark Zandi, told Globes in May that Israel *has "one of the world's best economies."* Elaborating, Zandi notes that Israel's *"fiscal situation is better than ever, the debt-to-GDP ratio is low and continues to fall, your economy has been growing for 15 straight years, and there's almost no unemployment."*

So who is being hurt by the BDS movement? The Palestinians, of course.

"The sanctions do run the risk of hurting the Palestinian economy," Lindow noted, *"which is much smaller and poorer than that of Israel."* The campaign against SodaStream, for example, may have made activists abroad feel good, but it was devastating to the hundreds of Palestinians who were sadly fired when the company moved its factory from Maale Adumim to the Negev.

BDS LIES ABOUT WOMEN'S ISSUES.

The moral bankruptcy of BDS campaigning is evident in women's rights issues. In early December, 2015, the National Women's Studies Association decided to link with BDS. How frivolously shallow their posturing is in their radical left-wing attitude that claims Jewish women living over the *'Green Line'* cannot be considered feminists. In other words, the values and ideology of such women are based on where they live. One step to the right and they are out. One step to the left and they are included. What utter tripe have these BDS-infected feminist activists adopted? What a brainless message they have in their violent cause?

They propagate a language in which Israelis are the aggressors and Palestinians are the weak defenseless victims, as if this has anything to do with women's issues. What nonsense!

In what moral universe is a young Jewish girl, attacked by a knife-wielding Palestinian Arab, the aggressor, and the Arab terrorist the weak one?

Do they have no rule of morality beyond the adoption of vacuous BDS slogans? Is that the depth of their value system?

Where is the oppression of women and girls in Palestinian society in their moral attitudes? It is ignored, as is the plain fact that Israel is the champion, throughout the whole of the Middle East and beyond, of women and feminine rights.

If the American National Women's Studies Association went looking for genital mutilation, honor killings, a sex slave industry, family rape, gender inequality, lesbian persecution in Israeli society they won't find any.

I suggest they do their job and begin to highlight these abuses in the surrounding Arab and Muslim countries, starting within Palestinian society.

I love Edgar Davidson. That is to say, I love his writing style. I don't know the man. I've never met him, but we are kindred spirits. Like me, he shines the spotlight on the hypocrisy of the anti-Israeli idiots and the sheer nonsense of their language. I have added a couple of examples of Edgar's brilliant work to this book. I do so with my recommendation that you find your way to his blog and discover other gems.

RULES & GUIDELINES FOR WESTERN MEDIA REPORTING ON ISRAEL.

This is the rule book to be issued to all members of the Western media corps. However, where these were intended only as guidelines, several news outlets including the BBC, CNN, Sky News, the Sun, Guardian, Independent, Times, have taken them so literally that I have had to issue formal complaints of plagiarism:

Rule 1 (Rocket attacks against Israel)

The rule here is simple: Never report on any rocket attacks against Israel. There are only two exceptions to this rule:

1. If Israel eventually attempts to stop the rocket fire. In that case, you can lead with a major story reporting that Israel has launched a massive attack against Palestinian civilians and you can include the following statement at the end of your 26 page report:

   "The Israelis claim that their attack was in response to homemade rocket attacks from Gaza/Lebanon."

2. If, as is common, the rockets fall short or explode while being launched causing casualties in Gaza, then you must write a major report with the headline *"Israeli attack kills 'X' civilians in Gaza."* The number *'X'* is determined by Rule 2 below.

Also note the following:

- If you are forced to mention Hamas and/or Hezbollah rockets, many of which are powerful long range missiles provided by Iran and Syria, you must refer to them using the terms: *"homemade"*, *"harmless"*, and *"nothing more than fire crackers"*.

- You may also say things like *"rockets were intercepted by the Iron Dome system"* so that it is not clear where the rockets were fired from, or by whom. However, if you do mention the Iron Dome system, ensure you say that it is an *"American supplied system"* even though it was actually funded, designed and built by Israel's Rafael Advanced Defense Systems.

- Never mention the fact that the missiles cause deaths, injuries, and major damage in Israel and require several million people in Israel to stay in shelters for hours and days on end.

Rule 2 (Arab casualties)

If there is any incident either in Israel or near its borders in which there are claims of Arab casualties you must write a report with the following headline: *"Israelis kill 'X' Arab civilians including 'Y' children"*

For the numbers 'X' and 'Y' simply choose the highest figures from the following sources:

- Hamas
- Hezbollah
- The Palestinian Authority
- Islamic Jihad
- Syrian State Television
- Islamic State
- Al Jazeera or Press TV
- Any person within 20 miles of the incident who is wearing a kaffiya or a Burka.

You are not required to state the source of your claim. In the unlikely event that an Israeli spokesman claims either a different figure or that the *'victims'* were armed terrorists, or that the incident simply did not happen, you may end your report with the following:

"An Israeli spokesman claimed that they 'acted in self-defense'."

An important note! In circumstances where Palestinian Arabs kill each other this should not be reported at all. This applies in cases where there is;

- Mass slaughter in fighting between different rival groups (Shia v Sunni, Hamas vs PA, Hamas vs Al Qaeda, PA vs Islamic Jihad, etc.)
- Where the victims are accused of being Israeli collaborators.

If news of these killings does leak out into the Western media then simply write a brief statement including the words:

"The underlying cause of the violence was the oppressive Israeli occupation."

Rule 3 (Demographics)

Remember the following important demographics in any report, especially relating to casualties:

- Every Palestinian, especially every member of Hamas and Islamic Jihad, is a **civilian**. Those who appear in suicide videos armed with machine guns vowing to kill as many Jews as possible are simply civilians forced by the Israeli occupation into becoming **militants.**
- Any Palestinian under the age of 26 is a **child**.
- Any Palestinian under the age of 16 is a **baby**.
- Any Palestinian over the age of 32 is a **grandfather/grandmother**.
- Any Palestinian with any type of injury (including especially Hamas terrorists injured when launching attacks against Israel) is **disabled**.
- Every building in Gaza is a Hospital, School, Mosque, or a house filled exclusively with women and children.
- There are no Israeli *'civilians'* and certainly no Israeli *'children'*. They are either **soldiers** or **settlers**.

- Palestinian cities and towns are **refugee camps**.
- Israeli cities and towns are **settlements**.

Rule 4 (Palestinian terrorist attacks)

If Israelis are killed in a terrorist attack, treat this as an opportunity to take a vacation from reporting.

However, you should immediately return from your vacation if it is discovered that an Israeli family in Jerusalem is planning to build an extra bedroom to accommodate their new baby. In that case you should write a story with the headline, *"Israelis destroy chance of peace by announcing new West Bank settlement plans."*

At the end of the article you can use the following statement: *"An Israeli government spokesman claimed that the settlement plans were in response to what they claimed was a 'terrorist attack'."*

The only exceptions to this rule are as follows:

- If the terrorist was killed by Israeli security forces attempting to stop the slaughter then you may post a brief report with a very large headline saying *"Palestinian murdered by Israeli security forces in occupied West Bank"* (note that Tel Aviv can be considered part of the West Bank for such reporting).
- If the terror attack is successful, and the terrorist is killed or captured, under no circumstances must any of its victims be named. You should, however, seek quotes and photos from the terrorists' family members showing him/her to be a loving person who supported Real Madrid.
- In the event of a suicide bombing you may interview the suicide bomber's family and write a sympathetic piece stating how the bomber was driven to his/her actions by the Israeli occupation. Be careful to refer to the actual suicide bombing only in vague abstract terms, never mentioning the victims or their families.

- In the event of a particularly brutal terrorist attack, such as the slaughter of an entire family in their home in which a baby is decapitated, you can, if news of the attack reaches outside Israel, write a brief report with the following words:

"Although the Israelis claim that a terrorist attack occurred at 'X', it is more likely to have been the result of a disgruntled Thai worker, Jewish militants intent on sparking anti-Arab violence, or simply a family dispute."

Make sure you never mention the widespread celebrations that take place throughout the Palestinian territories. Instead you should quote a Palestinian Authority spokesman, who having just led the celebrations with proclamations such as *"This will be the fate of all Jews"* in Arabic, tells you in English that the Palestinian Authority do not approve of the attack as it damages their cause, and that in any case such actions are the natural response to the Israeli occupation.

Rule 5 (Jewish "terrorist" attacks)

- In contrast to the multiple Arab terrorist attacks that must not be reported, the extremely rare attacks that can be attributed to Jews must be given total and uninterrupted prominence, irrespective of importance of any other news story including the death of the Queen.
- Any rules we may have about not using the word *'terrorist'* and not using the religion of the person carrying out an attack can be ignored. The words *"Jewish terrorist(s)"* must appear in the headline and in the first sentence of every paragraph.
- No act of aggression should be considered too minor to report. This includes any acts against property (e.g. Hebrew graffiti sprayed on a mosque) and any physical contact by a Jew against any Arab. This is one area of reporting where you are allowed to listen to main stream Israeli reporters since they are especially eager to promote such stories widely.

- **Even when there is absolutely no evidence,** as in most cases, that the acts were carried out by Jews, you must never suggest that there may be any doubt about it. Again, you can follow main stream left-wing Israeli reporters since they are world-leaders in self-flagellation. The fact that 99% of all reported acts of *'Jewish terrorism'* turn out to have actually been committed by Arabs - either to incite violence or simply as part of local tribal feuds - must never be mentioned.

- Do not under any circumstances mention the fact that, in total contrast to Palestinians and their leaders who celebrate every terrorist attack against Jews and honor their terrorists, Israelis universally condemn any rare attack carried out by Jews.

- In addition to the story itself, make sure that there are several editorials with headings such as *"As a Jew I am ashamed of Israel"*, or *"If Israelis had any self-respect they would declare their state illegitimate and leave"*, or *"Right wing Israelis seek the murder of all Arabs"*, or *"Israel becomes a criminal state"*, or *"Jewish terrorism inevitable result of Israeli apartheid."*

Rule 6 (Terminology)

- The word *'terrorist'* must never be used except when referring to Jews (as in Rule 5) or to any Jew accused of acting provocatively in the presence of an Arab.

- Any Arab in a combat zone is **unarmed** if they are not carrying a missile launcher. Any kind of guns, knives, swords, rocks, sticks or heavy metal items are, as a matter of course, carried innocently by 'unarmed' Arabs since it is part of their cultural heritage.

- In any report you must insert the word *"settler"* after the word *"Israeli"*, unless it is known that they live outside of Central Tel Aviv, in which case you must add the word *"fanatical"* before *"Israeli"*.

- When mentioning the name of any Israeli city or town (i.e. settlement) you must also include the words *'occupied territory.'*

- When mentioning any Israeli politician you must insert the word *"hardline, "extremist,"* or *"right-wing"* before their name. If in doubt it is best to insert all three words.

- In any report about Palestinians use the following words: *"indigenous," "suffering,"* or *"poor".*

- When mentioning any Palestinian politician you must insert the word *"moderate"* before their name, even if they are a leader of Hamas, Islamic Jihad or Fatah.

- Be especially careful when referring to Arab-Israelis. If an Arab-Israeli is killed in a Palestinian terrorist attack, or in a cross border shooting/rocket attack then you must refer to them as *"Palestinian."* Be careful not to mention who caused the killing. In other circumstances you must refer to them as Israelis to ensure that nobody knows that there are Arab-Israeli citizens prominent and represented in all strata of Israeli society.

Rule 7 (Ethics and Morality)

- Israel is the only country in the world that must behave with absolutely perfect ethics and morality in every single aspect of public and private life. Hence, even the smallest deviation from perfection, such as finding an Arab worker earning less than a Jewish worker, or an Arab rioter being manhandled by a policeman, can be treated as a major news story.

- Arab countries, and especially the Palestinians, do not have to abide by any rules of morality or ethics at all. Hence, institutional antisemitism, violence, child abuse, racism, sexism, indoctrination of children, and the fact that 99.99% of the population dreams of massacring every Jew in the world are all examples of acceptable cultural behavior and so must never be reported. Doing so will result in you being disciplined for Islamophobia, or for being a Zionist stooge.

Rule 8 (Geography and Religion)

- Never look at a **map of the whole Middle East.** That way you will never have to reveal that Israel is less than the size of Wales or New Jersey surrounded by Muslim countries with a land mass over a thousand times larger.

- Although you can refer to the fact that 20% of Israel's population is Arab you should only do so if you include the words *"oppressed minority", "abused", "underclass", "impoverished".*

- Never ask why over 50% of Israel's *Jewish* population appears to have dark or even black skin. This might otherwise force you to reveal that not all Israeli Jews are of European/American origin and that they are actually native Middle Eastern or Ethiopian origin.

- Never ask why there are zero Jews living in Gaza, zero Jews living in the PA occupied part of the *"West Bank"*, zero Jews living in Jordan, zero Jews living in Syria (down from 16,000 in 1947), zero Jews living in Iraq (down from 200,000 in 1940), zero Jews living in Algeria (down from 150,000 in 1940), zero Jews living in Libya (down from 50,000 in 1940), zero Jews living in Lebanon (down from 10,000 in 1940), 30 Jews living in Egypt (down from 100,000 in 1940), 2000 Jews living in Morocco (down from 270,000 in 1940), zero Jews living in Saudi Arabia, etc. Do, however, say that Israel's policies make it an apartheid state committed to ethnic cleansing of all Arabs.

- Never ask why Israel is the only country in the Middle East whose Christian population is growing.

- Never ask why Jerusalem is mentioned over 600 times in the Old Testament and not once in the Koran. Do, however, refer at least once in every report to the fact that Jerusalem is sacred to Muslims.

Rule 9 (Using photographs)

- Any photo that you find of dead children in conflict from anywhere in the world must be posted immediately to Twitter with the caption *"New evidence that Israel murders babies for fun"*. Photos of victims from the civil wars in Syria and Iraq are an especially good source. You do not have to worry even if they are over 10 years old. You may even use stills from horror films.

- Since Arabs/Muslims are **always** the victims and Israelis are **always** the aggressors any photograph showing: Muslims attacking Jews, dead or injured Jews, damage to Israeli property from Muslim violence or rockets, can all be assumed to be faked and must never be shown. There is one exception to this rule and that is if the photograph does not obviously identify Muslims as the aggressors and Jews as the victim. In that case you are allowed to show the photograph with an appropriate caption making it clear that Jews are the aggressors and Muslims the victims.

- If at any time you cannot find relevant photos that can be used to portray Israel as aggressor and Arabs as victim, then simply. You can either just doctor existing photos or better still create your own scene using the ever obliging Palestinians. If you have no volunteers then simply find a pile of rubbish anyway and place a child's toy or doll on the top. This enables you to tweet a photo with the caption *"all that remains of nursery destroyed by Israel"*. Other variations of this are to place a broken wheelchair on top and use the caption *"all that remains of disabled people's home destroyed by Israel"*.

Rule 10 (Speaking to the natives)

Never interview an Israeli Jew (Israeli Arabs, especially those belonging to the Islamic Movement can be used instead). The only exceptions to this rule are:

- Haaretz reporters

- Anti-Zionist academics, writers, politicians and lawyers
- Amos Oz
- Any recent American Jewish immigrant living in the West Bank who uses Biblical quotations every other sentence.

To ensure this rule is adhered to it is safest to simply never speak to any Israeli Jew. Hence, make sure that whenever you are in Israel you either stay in the (Arab) American Colony Hotel in Jerusalem or are hosted by a member of the Palestinian Authority or a person with a Haaretz press pass.

Rule 11 (Peace activists)

Any non-Arab in the region who is involved in violent anti-Israel activities is a **peace activist**. If such a person dies under any circumstances then you must state before any evidence is produced that this person *"was killed by Israeli occupying forces."* You must also put out an urgent call to all journalists in the world to write about nothing else for the next 7 days. Also contact every playwright to request a play dedicated to this martyr of the Palestinian cause.

Rule 12 (Arabic speeches)

Never use the services of an Arabic translator to find out what Arab leaders and clerics are telling their own people, as in *"We will not rest until every Jew is dead."* This will ensure you do not have to waste time telling readers that they have directly contradicted what they told you in English (as in *"We want peace"*). It will also save you having to explain (or even report) that wild anti-Semitic conspiracy theories are believed by 99.999% of all Arabs. A simple rule of thumb is the following:

Any statement made to you by an Arab in English (X) is to be treated as unimpeachable truth. Any statement made by an Arab in Arabic that contradicts X, can be treated as false and hence ignored.

In the unlikely event that news of the translation gets into the main stream media you simply report that the translation is the work of MEMRI – a Zionist organization dedicated to mis-translation to make Arabs look like anti-Semitic, homophobic, misogynistic psychopaths. If, even after that, the translation is proven to be accurate then you can simply say that the statement was *"the words of a distressed and oppressed Palestinian which was never supposed to be meant literally"*.

Rule 13 (Israeli evidence)

Be aware that in most major stories where you are able to cast Israel as the devil incarnate will result in the Israelis subsequently producing hard evidence (videos, documents, etc.) that prove they were not guilty of the claims made against them. In such cases there is no need to report this evidence. However, if you wish to remind readers of the original story you can include the following words at the end:
"Israel claimed that some of the accusations are not true, but sources cast doubt on the authenticity of the Israeli evidence."

Rule 14 (Tactics of War)

- Targeted assassinations of terrorists carried out by Israelis are, under all circumstances, **heinous war crimes**. When reporting such crimes always use the words **widespread international condemnation** and invoke the specter of a UN Security Council resolution. Never mention that the targeting of the terrorist was carried out with such careful planning and skill that no civilian was harmed during the operation. Also never mention the direct threat the terrorist posed to Israel, nor the Israelis previously killed by the terrorist.

- Targeted assassinations of terrorists carried out by any country other than Israel are, under all circumstances, **causes for jubilation**. When reporting such crimes always use the words **widespread international support** although you can include the words *"concern expressed by some Muslim militants."* Never mention the fact that, unlike assassinations carried out by

Israel, dozens of innocent civilians were also killed. Also never mention the fact that, unlike when Israel targets terrorists, the terrorist did not pose a direct threat to the country carrying out the attack.

- Never mention the fact that in Palestinian suicide terrorist attacks, children are always specifically targeted. Just stress that such attacks are the inevitable result of the *'occupation'* and *'poverty.'*

- The total blockading of a country's borders and carpet bombing of its cities by nations from the other side of the world (as in the West against Libya in 2011) is a highly commendable tactic even though the country poses no threat to its neighbors. Stress the tyrannical nature of the regime being bombed (and do not remind readers that, six months earlier, you were telling them what a wonderful reformer their leader was) and never remind readers about the civilians living there (who mostly hate the regime).

- The blockading of Gaza's sea border to stop weapons deliveries, and the targeted bombing of its terror facilities by its neighbor (Israel) who the Gazans have shelled indiscriminately, is a heinous war crime, that must be the subject of multiple UN resolutions, enquiries, and *'peace'* flotillas. Never mention the tyrannical nature of the Hamas regime, but focus only on the civilians living there without mentioning that they support the regime and all rejoice in the deaths of Israeli citizens. You should also point out the *'hypocrisy of the West'* in not imposing a no-fly zone on Israel.

Rule 15 (Peace Partners)

Under no circumstances ever mention that the Hamas Charter calls for the death of all Jews and cites the Protocols of the Elders of Zion for its inspiration. Similarly, never mention that, even after the Oslo accords, the Palestinian Authority has never renounced its own charter calling for the destruction of Israel and that every one of its leaders openly seeks the destruction of the Jewish State.

Rule 16 (Writing feature-length insight articles)

This is covered by Daniel Greenfield in *"How to write about Israel."*

Rule 17 (The Final Option)

If you have any doubt about the content of a story, or if you simply cannot be bothered to write anything yourself, then simply copy and paste whatever Al Jazeera or Press TV is saying on its website.

IS ANTI-ZIONISM THE SAME AS ANTI-SEMITISM?

Apparently one of the worst accusations you can make against anti-Zionists (such as Jeremy *"not an anti-Semitic bone in his body"* Corbyn, Livingstone, Galloway, Warsi, Alibi Brown, etc.) is that they are anti-Semitic.

The following chart attempts to clarify the differences between anti-Semitism and anti-Zionism. Clearly the two things have absolutely nothing in common;

	Antisemitism	Anti-Zionism
Basic Definition	Hatred of Jews.	Hatred of the Jewish state.
Core belief 1	Unlike all other people, the Jews are not entitled to equal rights.	Unlike all other people, the Jews are not entitled to self-determination in their own state.
Core belief2	The Jews are the root cause of most of the world's problems.	The Jewish state is the root cause of most of the world's problems.
What vociferous proponents want	Physical destruction of the entire Jewish race.	Physical destruction of the entire Jewish state.
What it based on	The singling out and demonization of Jews – and Jews alone -	The singling out and demonization of the Jewish state – and the

	based on a set of complete lies about the political, economic, social and religious behavior of Jews.	Jewish state alone - based on a set of complete lies about the political, economic, social and religious behavior of the Jewish state.
How is it currently sustained	Continued, incessant lies and propaganda about Jews – much of it from Muslim countries, Soviets and Western academia, promulgated in the media and on the web, that is rarely if ever challenged.	Continued, incessant lies and propaganda about the Jewish State – much of it from Muslim countries, Soviets and Western academia, promulgated in the media and on the web, that is rarely if ever challenged.
Typical media presentation	Cartoons of big fat Jews who control the world and eat non-Jewish babies; cartoons of Jews killing non-Jewish children.	Cartoons of big fat Jews who control the world and eat non-Jewish babies; cartoons of Jewish soldiers killing Arab children.
Who currently are the most virulent proponents Jewish proponents?	Muslims, left-wing political activists, Black panthers, right-wing extremists, racists, self-hating Jews. In Muslim countries Pew surveys report 96% of the population 'hate Jews.' Those whose only connection to Judaism is when they say "As a	Muslims, left-wing political activists, Black panthers, right-wing extremists, racists, self-hating Jews. In Muslim countries Pew surveys report 98% of the population 'hate Israel.' Those whose only connection to Judaism is when they say "As a Jew

	Jew I deplore the Jewish religion."	I deplore the Jewish state."
Most common beliefs	Jews are baby-killers; Jews did 9/11 Jews control the media Jews control America, Britain, France (add any country you like, including even Arab ones) like Jews control the world banking system, the United Nations (add any international organization you like) Jews bake the blood of Christian children in their Passover matzos; Jews are behind ISIS Jews are racists – they discriminate against non-Jews.	Zionists are baby-killers; Zionists did 9/11 Zionists control the media Zionists control America, Britain, France (add any country you like, including even Arab ones) like Zionists control the world banking system, the United Nations (add any international organization you like) Zionists bake the blood of Arab children in their Passover matzos; Zionists are behind ISIS The Jewish State is racist/Apartheid – it discriminates against non-Jews.
Tactic 1: Delegitimization	The message that the Jews are a depraved, illegitimate, 'invented' race. Denial of Jewish history including its origin in the Middle East.	The message that the Jewish State is depraved, 'invented' and illegitimate. Denial of Jewish history including its origin in the Middle East.
Tactic 2: Boycott	In the 1930s the Nazi	The BDS campaign

	singled out Jews for economic, cultural, political, and academic boycott (antisemites still do this informally).	singles out the Jewish State (and Jews that support it) for economic, cultural, political, and academic boycott.
Economic boycott in practice	Boycott Jewish businesses, products and services; vandalize Jewish-owned shops and their products, including daubing Swastikas and Stars of David.	Boycott Jewish owned Israeli businesses, products and services; vandalize Jewish-owned Israeli shops and their products, including daubing Swastikas and Stars of David.
Cultural boycott in practice	In Nazi Germany Jewish artists, performers, writers and sportsmen were not allowed to perform, while books, art, and plays sympathetic to Jews were banned.	Jewish Israeli artists, performers, writers and sportsmen are not allowed to perform, while books, art, and plays sympathetic to the Jewish state are shut out or shut down.
Use of the Law	In the 1930s special Nazi laws introduced to both outlaw Jewish-owned businesses and criminalize attempts by anybody else to work with them.	Special EU and Arab laws introduced to outlaw Jewish-owned Israeli businesses and criminalize attempts by anybody else to work with them.
Secondary boycott tactics	In Nazi Germany, Non-Jews doing business with Jews were publicly vilified and threatened to be boycotted if they did	Non-Jews doing business with the Jewish state are publicly vilified and threatened to be boycotted if they do not cease their

	not cease their interaction with Jews.	interaction with the Jewish state.
Labelling and taxes	The Nazis forced Jews to wear the yellow star while Muslim countries have always forced Jews to pay a 'dhimmi' tax.	The EU forces Israel to put special labels on goods produced by Jewish-owned businesses in places like Jerusalem.
Typical everyday behavior	Criticizing Jews for certain character traits (such as meanness, aggressiveness, deviousness) that are actually far more prominent in most other ethnic and religious groups Criticizing Jews for their genuinely good character traits (such as intelligence, technology skills and business acumen) as in *"The Jews use these traits to trick and steal from non-Jews."*	Criticizing the Jewish State for certain character traits (such as meanness, aggressiveness, deviousness) that are actually far more prominent in most other countries Criticizing the Jewish State for its genuinely good character traits (such as intelligence, technology skills and business acumen) as in *"The Zionists use these traits to trick and steal from the Arabs.'*
Beliefs about the Holocaust	The Holocaust is a myth perpetuated to gain sympathy for Israel. The only real holocaust was committed by Zionists against Palestinians.	The Holocaust is a myth perpetuated to gain sympathy for Israel. The only real holocaust was committed by Zionists against the Palestinians.
What especially angers proponents	Jews defending themselves from attack;	The Jewish state defending itself from attack;

	Any Jewish success in science and culture.	Any Israeli success in science and culture.
What they have never heard of or must never be mentioned	The total destruction of Jewish communities in Muslim lands after the establishment of Israel.	The total destruction of Jewish communities in Muslim lands after the establishment of Israel.
About the killing of Jews by Arab terrorists	If it really happens the Jews must have had it coming to them.	If it happens at all it is a natural reaction against Zionist crimes.
About violence generally	Jews are legitimate targets for violence.	Zionist Jews are legitimate targets for violence.
Who are their heroes	Hitler, George Galloway, Saddam Hussein, Iran and any other bigots you can think of - because they "stood up to the Jews."	George Galloway, Saddam Hussein, Iran and any other bigot you can think of – because they "stood up to the ~~Jews~~ Zionists."
Mandatory reading	Protocols of the Elder of Zion, anything by Gilad Atzmon.	Protocols of the Elder of Zion, anything by Gilad Atzmon.
Popular phrase	"Jews go to Palestine."	"Jews out of Palestine."
What happens if their proponents 'win'	Millions of Jews were killed in the Holocaust, but it did not help the Nazis in any way at all.	Millions of Jews will be killed, but it will not help the Palestinians in any way at all.
Proponents most hated thing in the whole world	The State of Israel.	The State of Israel.

BDS LIES ABOUT GAZA.

It is true there are stringent restrictions on what goes in or comes out of the Gaza Strip. This, sadly, is critically necessary due to the incessant violence radiating out of Gaza from Hamas and assorted terrorist groups that are based there.

The international community recognizes the restrictions as necessary and legal.

Despite this, eight hundred trucks a day flow into Gaza from Israel carrying everything from essential goods and supplies to luxury items. Over one and a half million tons of construction material has gone from Israel into Gaza at no small risk to the Jewish state as Hamas purloins the bulk of this material to build their terrorist infrastructure, including the underground terror attack and supply tunnels that plagued Israeli civilians during the 2014 war that Hamas launched against Israel. So sophisticated and extensive are the network of tunnels that IDF soldiers nicknamed them *"the Gaza Metro."*

But if the BDS want to complain about an *"illegal blockade on Gaza"* why have they said nothing about the Egyptian government. Nothing goes into Gaza from Egypt and Gazans are lucky to find the border crossing with Egypt open to them a very few times in a year and only for periods of 48 hours.

The Egyptians impose their restrictions on Gaza for the same reasons that Israel does. They discovered, to their cost, that Palestinian terrorists exploited their kindness to use their territories to launch terror attacks against their police, soldiers and against tourists visiting Egypt.

Egypt and Israel see eye to eye on the need to control and limit the behavior of a dangerous Hamas in Gaza.

ALTERNATIVES TO A FAILED TWO-STATE SOLUTION.

How much longer to we need to go to understand that Israel cannot be expected to survive in the ghetto into which the international community seems determined to drive the Jewish state?

How long must we plod our weary way along the desert of wishful thinking toward the distant oasis of two-states? Isn't fifty year and counting enough for us to realize that this oasis does not exist, that it is merely a shimmering mirage, a Fanta-morgana, that drives desperately thirsty politicians and diplomats with fevered determination focused on an unreachable goal?

Isn't it time to appreciate why their persistency is doomed to failure and, instead, begin to discuss and consider alternatives to a failed two-state solution?

Israel can ill afford to restrict itself into the razor thin coastal plain that will be dominated by a hostile entity looking down on its main civilian population and essential commercial, residential, industrial and security infrastructures. Israel's one international airport, its military command and control centers, its national storage facilities, all would be within eye and missile range of recalcitrant enemy. The same enemy would be positioned in the streets and alleyways of Jerusalem in current Palestinian and international demands are met by Israel. Israel's strategic eastern border would not be the Jordan River. It would be a mere eight miles from the Mediterranean coastal town of Netanya, where I live, leaving my family and grandchildren just two miles from a potential Hamastan.

Sorry! This is not acceptable to me.

Although many in the international community are truly altruistic is their desire to find an equitable peace between Israelis and their Arab enemies, particularly those adopting a Palestinian garb, the vast majority of the Muslim world together with other malevolent nations view the Palestinian national aspirations as being a tactical maneuver designed to lead to the destruction of the Jewish State of Israel.

This is absolutely true of the BDS Movement as espoused by their leader, Omar Barghouti, and thousands of supporters of the Palestinian cause who, in their chants and slogans, are passionate about the end of Israel being the necessary precursor to the establishment of the State of Palestine *"from the river to the sea."*

Consider the compelling words of Martin Sherman, head of the Israel Institute for Strategic Studies.

"A dispassionate evaluation of the events of the past decades inexorably compels one toward an increasingly evident conclusion: The Palestinians seem far more focused on annulling Jewish political independence than attaining Palestinian political independence, for more committed to deconstruction of the Jewish state than to construction of a Palestinian one.

In spite of almost universal international endorsement of their claims, highly supportive international media coverage, decades of super power patronage, enormous international financial aid, highly accommodative Israeli regimes which not only acknowledged but identified with their claims, the Palestinians have failed miserably in establishing any semblance of a stable, productive self-governing society or producing any capable, credible, and competent leadership likely to advance them along the path towards the goal. Indeed, they have, instead, the corrupt kleptocracy of Fatah, the tyrannical theocracy of Hamas and the chronic chaos of the Palestinian Authority.

In this sense, the Palestinians, by their manifest inability to achieve statehood despite the highly conducive conditions that prevailed in the favor, appear to have failed the test of history thereby casting severe doubt as to whether they are worthy of such statehood.

But even if one is convinced that the Palestinians are underserving of a state, the question still remains as to whether they are genuinely desirous of one. In this regard, there are two competing, indeed antithetical, hypotheses by which to explain the Israeli-Palestinian conflict and the motivations behind it.

According to the first of these hypotheses, the fuel of the conflict is the lack of Palestinian self-determination, and all that the Palestinians aspire to is the establishment of their own state. There is, however, an alternative explanation whereby the fuel of the conflict is not the lack of Palestinian self-determination but the existence of Jewish self-determination, and that as long as Jewish self-determination persists, so will the conflict. Moreover, according to this alternative explanation, the goal of the Palestinians is not to establish a state for themselves but to dismantle a state for others – the Jews.

Accordingly, further pursuit of a Palestinian state is likely to prove both futile and detrimental. For, as past precedents strongly suggest, it will advance neither peace nor prosperity, but only serve as a platform for further violence against Israel."

One only need look at Gaza to see how true Sherman's words are. Israel made the ultimate demonstrational gesture for peace with the Palestinians by the withdrawal from territory and the removal of thousands of Israelis from every settlement in the Gaza Strip in 2005. Israel left behind fertile land and rich agricultural facilities as a further gift to the Palestinians to enter into the Strip and continue the path to peace and good neighborliness. Can anyone put their hand on their heart and say that the Palestinians reciprocated constructively in a way that benefitted their own people and assured Israel that they accepted the notion of a peaceful state alongside their Jewish neighbors? Instead, they constructed an Islamic Frankenstein called Hamastan that exploited and robbed its own people of hope, peace and prosperity while calling for the death of Israel and set out to kill and torment Jews.

Name me one national movement that contains the following message in its founding document;

"The time will not come until Muslims will fight the Jews and kill them, until the Jews hide behind rocks and trees which will cry, 'Oh Muslim! There is a Jew hiding behind me. Come out and kill him!"

I can only think of one – Nazi Germany, as expressed by Hitler in his *'Mein Kampf.'* Or maybe there is one more – Iran, with its national ambition to wipe Israel off the map and mob chants of *"Death to Israel."*

Read that sentence which is Article Seven from the infamously anti-Semitic Hamas Charter and tell me if it is possible to put this aside and withdraw from even more crucially important territory that will, inevitably, fall to a determined Hamas.

HAMAS FLAGS FLYING OVER JERUSALEM.

Mahmoud Abbas said, on 11 November 2012, that Palestinians *"would continue the march until victory when Palestinian flags are hoisted over the walls of the Old City of Jerusalem and its mosques and churches."*

As if this thought wasn't bad enough, notice he did not say anything about synagogues, or other Jewish holy places. In case you were wondering, this has nothing to do with his respect for our sacred sites. He hasn't got any, if we are to believe what official Palestinian TV News is saying.

The *Palestine Media Watch* NGO, headed by Itamar Marcus, exposed an item in which the Palestinian Authority denounced the existence of any Jewish history in Jerusalem. In this report, they claimed that the Jewish Temple *"exists only in the minds of radical organizations."*

Not only do they deny Jewish identity to Jerusalem and the land, they actively reject and destroy all evidence and facts placed in front of them, as they did by excavating under the Temple Mount, smashing the artefacts into tiny pieces of rubble and dumping it into the Kidron Valley. In its place, they invent an ancient Palestinian history unprovable by any physical evidence. The Palestinian Authority, from Abbas down, accuses Israel of stealing Palestinian heritage when confronted with the evidence of Jewish history. So what hope is there for mutual understanding and recognition? There is none.

What does a Palestine look like with its new capital located in east Jerusalem? What do Palestinian flags flying over Jerusalem mean in real estate terms? And what are the potentially explosive repercussions of such a move? Would they be hoisted over the Temple Mount and the Western Wall as a defiant gesture to Jews at prayer?
They have already said they do not recognize such places. What about David's Citadel, or the Hurva Synagogue? Will you be willing to stand in Mamilla as Jews are expelled from their homes in the Old City and eastern

parts of Jerusalem, and see Palestinian, even Hamas, flags flying over the walls of the Old City and the Zion Gate? Apparently, those who support the division of Jerusalem would. They naïvely think this would herald peace.

The battle for real estate comes down to this. Can you see Hadassah Hospital and the Rockefeller Museum under the sovereignty of a Palestinian Authority, possibly led by Hamas? Will Christians, worldwide, tolerate having the Garden of Gethsemane and the Church of the Holy Sepulcher in the hands of the Palestinians, probably Hamas? Do they care, at all, who will be the future guardians of their holy shrines? How about the Mount of Olives? And here's the clincher. Even if Israel were to be naïve enough to hand over this real estate to Palestinians, will we be able to live with ourselves, will be able to live, when Hamas takes over the feeble Palestinian Authority and rule over these vital assets in the heart of Jerusalem?

What would we have sacrificed for peace when that day comes, as it inevitably will?

Will we see the Islamic flag, alongside the Palestinian one, flying over sacred Jewish and Christian sites, announcing yet another conquest in their regional and global crusade?

To those who think that Hamas is confined to the Gaza Strip, allow me to disillusion you.

In April 2015, students at Bir Zeit University gave Hamas an overwhelming victory in the election of a new students union. We need to remind ourselves that Bir Zeit is not in the Gaza Strip. It is located within touching distance of Ramallah where the Palestinian Authority is based. It would be wrong to think of Bir Zeit as a radical campus. Until now, it was considered as representing the Palestinian street.

At a future point in time we will realize, too late, that our *"peace gesture"* was, in reality, our surrender and submission to their will.

In that day, will the Hebrew University be renamed the Islamic University? Surely it is better to live with their *"Nakba"* than to perpetrate our own?

As if this wasn't bad enough, in June 2012, an Egyptian cleric, in an shocking display of Islamic chutzpah, claimed Jerusalem will be the capital of Egypt under Muslim Brotherhood rule. Safwat Hagazy said on Egyptian *Annas TV*,

"Our capital shall not be Cairo, Mecca, or Medina. It shall be Jerusalem, with Allah's will. Our chant will be 'millions of martyrs will march towards Jerusalem!'"

I wonder what the Palestinians think about their new capital overrun by an emerging Egypt?

What he meant was that Jerusalem is to be the center of an Islamic global Caliphate, achieved on the back of the Palestinian movement, even if they have to conquer it by force. He proved this by adding,

"Yes. We will either pray in Jerusalem, or we will be martyred there!"

Masked rioters have already been seen carrying the green Hamas flag through the streets of Jerusalem. Better to give it peacefully to the Palestinians and avoid the bloodshed, we are told. No self-respecting Jew would tolerate this heinous scenario.

All this is not to say we should cease striving for a solution to the Palestinian problem, if only to get them off our backs. It may take the form of a Two-State Solution. It may take other forms. Clearly, after decades of failure, it will require creative, even original, thinking. Perhaps a Two-State Solution is not the answer? Despite the overwhelming opinion that this, and only this, is the only game in town, it is obviously not happening, despite the billions being pumped into the corrupt, incompetent, rejectionist Palestinian leadership, despite the tremendous pressure being put on Israel.

How can it be, given our negotiating partner? Who, on the other side, can deliver a final and permanent peace acceptable to Jews and to clear thinking Christians, even if Israel were to give them everything they want?

Who, in fact, speaks for the Palestinians – all the Palestinians? Answer - no one.

So let's stop dreaming and get real. Let's not waste time trying to persuade a weak, cowardly, rejectionist, and devious leader of a Palestinian minority who, according to local elections in the West Bank, failed to secure majorities in any of the main towns and cities, including Ramallah. The Palestinians refuse to recognize the Jewish state or the desire to live in peace alongside us. And Hamas, the popular choice of the Palestinian street, is infinitely worse. Palestinian Arabs, beyond Abbas's parochial parish area, have no intention of settling for anything less than the elimination of the Zionist entity. Let's be brutally honest, even Abbas shares that dream, despite rhetoric to the contrary.

It is clear, from their public incitement and declarations, that none of them have any desire to live alongside Israel in peace and harmony. On the contrary, as we constantly witness, they really want to kill us.

A people whose bible doesn't mention Jerusalem once, a people who, when they pray in Jerusalem, do so with their backsides facing the Temple Mount and the Dome of the Rock, cannot claim Jerusalem as a capital based on religious grounds, despite their protests.
In truth, they want it as a statement of conquest, to plant their flag to displace the Jewish infidel's sovereignty over Jerusalem. It's less about having their state. It's more about destroying our state and planting their victory flag over Jerusalem.

Planting a flag is a sign of sovereignty, but sovereignty over what? Will it be a state or a staging post? Here's what Yasser Arafat said back in 1993;

"...the Palestinian state is within our grasp. Soon the Palestinian flag will fly on the walls, the minarets and the cathedrals of Jerusalem. Since we cannot defeat Israel in war, we do this in stages. We take any and every territory that we can of Palestine, and establish sovereignty there, and we use it as a springboard to take more. When the time comes, we can get the Arab nations to join us for the final blow against Israel."

Interesting to note that he said this on the same day he signed the Declaration of Principles on the White House lawn alongside President Clinton and Israeli Prime Minister, Yitzchak Rabin.

Such is the deception of the Palestinians. Can we believe that Mahmoud Abbas, raised in the spirit of Arafat, is any different? Jerusalem is the springboard to the rest of Israel.

Mahmoud Abbas holds to the same desire as Hamas who recently declared, during their recent missile attack on Israel;

"We are announcing a war against the sons of apes and pigs, which will not end until the flag of Islam is raised in Jerusalem."

Presently, it's time for crisis management, not crisis solutions. In politics, as in business, you should only enter into crisis solutions when you are absolutely sure that everyone gathered around the table is ready, honest, and capable of delivering an acceptable permanent agreement. Do we have that with the Palestinians? No.

Given a referendum, the majority of Israelis would readily accept a pragmatic and guaranteed end of conflict agreement given an adversary willing to live in peace with Israel. Nobody can claim this to be true about the other side. Crisis solution, therefore, is out of the question when the opposing proponent is a minority representative of a fractious society and has proven incapable of uniting his people around him. Hence, crisis management and original alternatives must be the order of the day.

The accumulation of evidence based on reality, or realpolitik, can only lead us to be wary of being led by the politically naïve wishful-thinkers into positions even more dangerous to Israel than we find ourselves today.

Truth be told, Israel finds itself trapped in a cleft-stick of its own making. Wishing to look magnanimous and willing to make peace gestures, it allowed arch-terrorist Yasser Arafat to be released from his isolation and exile in Tunis and to be welcomed back into the area where he spat on the Oslo Accords, which was his passport back to Ramallah, and recommenced his murderous campaign of death against innocent Israelis.

Following Arafat's death in 2004, Prime Minister Sharon, decided to evacuate every Israeli from the Gaza Strip. Israelis have been haunted by the consequences of this *'peace'* action.

The reality on the ground forces another metaphor on us. That we have walked into a dangerous cul-de-sac. We have tried to talk to the enemy into accepting us and they have showed us in no uncertain manner that they mean us harm.

So, no! We will not make the gesture that will result in Hamas flags flying over Jerusalem.

If you want to hear three lies in four words, try *"illegally, occupied, Palestinian land."*

It's not illegal, it's not occupied, and it's not Palestinian land.

Now, let's talk!

BDS LIES ABOUT ISRAELI SOLDIERS.

BDS LIES when they call our brave soldiers *"war criminals"* and accuse the IDF of *"war crimes."* So let me introduce non-Israel, non-Jewish neutral military experts to give their opinion.

14 international former chiefs of staff and senior military officers reviewed the 2014 Gaza conflict from both the IDF and Hamas operations.

They visited Israel both during and after the conflict. They interviewed soldiers from the regular foot-soldiers to unit commanders all the way up to the highest ranks of the IDF. In their fact finding missions they also spoke with military intelligence personnel.

While conducting in-depth analysis into Operation Protective Edge they received unprecedented access to the IDF and to government officials up to the Prime Minister that, together with their impeccable military expertise, enabled them to produce a fair and factual report which they released in early December 2015.

They began by admitting that Israel's military efforts were entirely necessary and justified in the defense of Israel's national security as a result of the aggressive and offensive operations conducted against Israeli civilian centers by Hamas and their other terror affiliates in support of Palestinian Hamas actions initiated against Israel.

Their conclusions solidly stated that *"Israel's conduct in the 2014 Gaza Conflict met and in some respects exceeded the highest standards we set for our own nation's militaries."*

They went on, *"It is our view that Israel fought an exemplary campaign, adequately conceived with appropriately limited objectives, displaying both a very high level of operational capability as well as a total commitment to the Laws of Armed Conflict."*

To emphasize the point, the report states, *"The IDF not only met its obligations under the Law of Armed Conflict, but often exceeded these on the battlefield at significant tactical costs, as well as in the humanitarian relief efforts that accompanied its operation."*

Additionally highlighting the conduct of the IDF and the Israeli soldier the report recorded that, *"Where the high standards of conduct the IDF sets for its personnel have not been met incidents are investigated, including criminal investigations, through an independent mechanism under the oversight of the democratic institutions of the State of Israel. This mechanism clearly meets the requirements of legal recourse, judicial independence and democratic oversight that our own nations set for ourselves."*

The team of overseas military experts reported on Hamas thus,

"Hamas not only flagrantly disregarded the Law of Armed Conflict as a matter of course as part of its terrorist-army hybrid strategic concept, but rather it abused the very protections afforded by the law for military advantage. It embedded its entire military machinery in civilian locations and sensitive sites, including those of the United Nations.

Hamas indiscriminately targeted Israeli civilians throughout the conflict with extensive rocket fire and willfully sought to draw the IDF into battle in a prepared urban stronghold amid the Palestinian civilian population in Gaza, for which it located its operational headquarters in Gaza's main hospital."

All these are war crimes.

The notable military staffers who researched and investigated the conflict included;

Colonel Richard Kemp; Commander of British Forces in Afghanistan. He also served in Iraq, the Balkans, South Asia and Northern Ireland. He led the international terrorism team at the UK's Joint Intelligence Committee and served as Chairman of the strategic intelligence group for COBRA, UK's national crisis management committee.

General Klaus Dieter Naumann; Former Chief of Staff of the German Armed Forces and served as Chairman of the NATO Military Committee from 1996 to 1999.

General Vincenzo Camporini; Former Italian Chief of Defense. He later served as Chief of Staff of the Italian Air Force as well as Chief of Defense General Staff.

Lt. General David A. Deptula; Former three-star general in the US Air Force. He was the principal attack planner for the Desert Storm coalition air campaign in 1991 and served as Director of the Combined Air Operations Center in Afghanistan and as first Deputy Chief of Staff for Intelligence, Surveillance and Reconnaissance at Air Force Headquarters.

Admiral Jose Maria Teran; Serves in the Office of Strategic Assessment of the Spanish Defense Minister and Former Chief of Joint Staff and Chief of the Strategic Analysis Group.

Major-General Andrew James Molan served as the Chief of Operations for the HQ Multinational Force in Iraq. Former Commander of the Australian Defense College.

Other top military leaders in the High Level International Military Group came from India, France and Columbia.

Lost in the malediction of cynical media misreporting and malevolent anti-Israel propaganda disguised as Palestinian human rights concerns is the fact that, during fifty days of war, Palestinian fired 4,564 rockets at Israeli civilian targets. Despite the UN statistics, which were adopted lies provided by the Palestinian Ministry of Health, de factor Hamas in Gaza, the real Gazan casualty figures show that 60% were men of fighting age, that many of the *"children"* quoted in the false figures were actually men in their 20s, that many Gazans were killed by Palestinian rockets aimed at Israel short-falling within Gaza and there is video evidence of Hamas conducting public executions of non-compliant Palestinians.

My investigations into Gaza casualty figures, conducted while the conflict was taking place and in the months after, confirmed the findings of these fourteen military experts that the Gaza casualty figures were remarkably low when taking into consideration the intensity of the fighting in such a densely populated area.

Consider this scenario. The Israeli Air Force conducted over 5000 sorties over Gaza, IDF artillery mapped out and targeted large concentrations of terrorist activity throughout the Gaza Strip, tanks softened up intense areas of terrorist strongholds in urban areas in preparation for the entry of thousands of infantry soldiers who were forced to destroy booby-trapped buildings alleyways and uncover and destroy miles of terror tunnels, rocket sites, and weapon storage facilities as well as fighting civilian-attired terrorists coming out of houses and public buildings to attack them. And yet there were only a few hundred non-combatants killed in such a ferocious and prolonged firefight. Any civilian killed in conflict is unfortunate, but this is a consequence of warfare and the Gaza war was imposed on Israel by Hamas. However, the actual loss of non-combatant lives in Gaza was markedly lower than similar combat situations conducted elsewhere.

As the international experts reported, this feat was achieved by both the accuracy of the surgical strikes of all elements of Israel's fighting force combined with the IDF humanitarian concern to avoid, as much as militarily possible, harming innocent civilians, even those in support of the Palestinian Hamas offensive against Israel.

SOME OF OUR CRASS ENEMIES ARE FELLOW JEWS.

It's not surprising to find Jews on the wrong side of the Israeli divide. After all, Jews have been on the wrong side of the political spectrum throughout the ages.

Jews became leading Catholic priests at the time of the Spanish Inquisition. They were some of the more prominent executioners of the heinous torture and murder against Spanish and Portuguese Jews.

Jews acted as kappos in the service of the Nazis in desperate efforts to save their own skins.

Jews led the Soviet Communist movement that led to the slaughter of millions.

So why should be expect anything different when radical far-left Jews decide to turn against the Jewish state?

This is how and why Peter Beinart can address the young participants at the 2015 JStreet Conference and implore them to put themselves in harm's way by joining Palestinian riots. It's part of the *'progressive'* ideology of *'ending the occupation.'* Their opposition to 'settlements' allows them to support Palestinian violence as legitimate *'resistance against Israeli occupation.'*

They think they are doing it out of altruistic, humanitarian, considerations. What is not considered is Israel's right to hold firm to territories, according to signed agreements with the Palestinians, until such time as there is a permanent peace agreement.

What fails to be included in their narrative is that much of the territory that Israel controls as an integral part of these agreements will remain under Israeli control in any final peace agreement.

These naïve Jews are lobbying strongly for the establishment of a Palestinian state not only on land already handed over by Israel, but on land they insist that Israel must surrender to the Palestinian whose cause they advocate so vehemently. They do so without supporting the genuine fears of most Israelis that any such solution will lead to a West Bank Palestine led by a Palestinian Hamas leadership, or worse, adamantly locked into the slaughter of Jews and the elimination of what will be left of Israel. Their sloganeering has no room for Jewish fears. Their adamant demands on Israel increasingly take the form of crass intimidation.

Consider Dr. Marsha Ann Levine, a crass Jewish academic in support of BDS.

She is a senior research associate at the MacDonald Institute for Archaeological Institute at Cambridge University in the United Kingdom.

Her specialty is horse husbandry, but her passion is hitting on Israel and Israelis, including young Israeli teens with an interest in her subject. To the esteemed Dr. Levine even a 13 year old girl is fair game for her rude bullying.

Shachar Rabinovitch is that teenage Israeli with a love of horses. As part of her school project research she made the mistake of writing in her poor English to this to BDS Levine boor;

"Hello. My name is Shachar Rabinovitch and I am from Israel.

I'm doing research for school about horses and it would be great if you can answer a few questions that I will ask.

What ancient horses were the breeds of the horse breeds we know today?

How did ancient humans create new breeds, or keep the ones that existed?

What ancient horse breeds did humans use the most and what was their use?

Where did the ancient horse breeds live?

Thank you for reading my questions.

Shahar Rabinovitch."

The reply from the callous Levine was quick in coming. This was her reply;

"Dear Shachar Rabinovitch,

I'll answer your questions when there is peace for Palestinians in Palestine.

I am a member of Jews for Justice for Palestinians.

I support Boycott, Divestment, Sanctions.

You might be a child, but if you are old enough to write to me, you are old enough to learn about Israeli history and how it has impacted on the lives of Palestinian people.

Maybe your family has the same views as I do, but I doubt it. So I suggest you look at this link.

Yours sincerely,

Dr. Marsha Levine."

The attached link had nothing to do with horses. It had everything to do with the political indoctrination of this Jewish academic. That is how they practice academic exchange at Cambridge under Dr. Levine.

BDS idiots such as Levine project themselves to be humanists and really good and caring human beings. When it comes to hating Israel out of all proportion and with an exclusive laser-like malevolency, they show their real ugly face.

The callousness of Dr. Marsha Ann Levine is just one example of where Jews have lost their Jewish soul in the cause of Palestine.

Others who profess to oppose BDS are, nevertheless, damaging to Israel. Here is what Harvard law professor, Alan Dershowitz, had to say about the American Jewish group, J Street, in the Tablet magazine in August 2015;

"I think J Street has been the most damaging organization in American history against Israel. It has been the most damaging, more damaging than Students for Justice in Palestine [and] more damaging than the early anti-Zionist Council for Judaism. J Street has done more to turn young people against Israel than any organization in the whole of history. It will go down in history as one of the most virulent, anti-Israel organizations in the history of Zionism and Judaism. It has given cover to anti-Israel attitudes on campus and particularly its approach to Israel's self-defense."

Dershowitz fact-checked their press releases, dating back to the first day of their existence.

"I couldn't find a single one that praised Israel. How can you be as pro-Israel organization and not express any pro-Israeli views? It's absolutely shocking to me. Every release seemed to have a negative about Israel."

J Street claims to be pro-Israel but all of its actions and statements have been damaging to Israel and reflect the attacks of anti-Israel propaganda. As Daniel Gordis, senior fellow at Jerusalem's Shalem College said, *"it is one thing to put pro-Israel on your tag line. It's something different to be pro-Israel."*

J Street has a history of taking money from anti-Israel sources and denying it. They denied receiving funding from George Soros until its leader, Jeremy Ben Ami, was forced to admit he lied about receiving $750,000 from Soros's family.

Anti-Israel Jewish involvement spans the range from blatant hatred to cover up.

BDS LIES ABOUT THE PALESTINIAN LEADERSHIP.

Here's what they don't tell you.

I'm tired of the BDS bullshit about Gaza. Here are some economic facts about Gaza and the Palestinian leadership.

$2.1 billion of world aid is extorted from the people of Gaza by Hamas.

How about the wealth of the Hamas extorters?

Hamas chief in Gaza, Ismail Haniya, has a worth of $3.5 billion. He owns a 2,500 square meter plot of prime real estate in Gaza City. He also owns thirteen houses in Gaza registered in the names of his thirteen kids.

Khaled Maashal, joint boss of Hamas and unofficial foreign minister, lives the life of luxury in a 5 star hotel in wealthy Doha. He has an assessed worth of $2.6 billion.

In Gaza, Musa Abu Marzuk, one of the senior Hamas bosses, is estimated to be worth over $2.6 billion.

Currently, there are an estimated 1,243 Hamas millionaires in Gaza, as well as a further 1,450 almost millionaires.

The unemployment rate in Gaza is 29% with Hamas-controlled wages of Gaza workers averaging $2900.

As for Mahmoud Abbas, leader of the Palestinian Authority, he is estimated to be worth at least $100 million, according to Muhammad Rashid, the head of the Palestinian Investment Fund. He also owns a private palace. Under his crony leadership, his sons have also become millionaires.

In testimony at a hearing of the US House Committee on the Middle East entitled *"Chronic Kleptocracy: Corruption within the Palestinian political establishment,"* headed by Committee Chairman, Steven Chabot, it was claimed that Mahmoud Abbas used his position of power to line his own pockets and that of his cronies, including his sons, Yasser and Tareq.

Politician and businessman Mohammed Dahlan was banished from the Palestinian-controlled territories after he claimed that $1.3 billion vanished from the Palestinian Investment Fund since it was put under Abbas' control in 2005.

Where is the BDS outcry over Palestinian leaders robbing their people and the international community blind?

THE OPINION OF OTHERS.

HOWARD JACOBSON AND THE CLOSING OF THE ACADEMIC MIND.

Award winning author, Howard Jacobson, is perhaps Britain's greatest living literary writers. His mastery of words sets him apart. This is why he was the worthy recipient of the 2010 Man Booker Prize for his book *'The Finkler Question.'* His literary genius shortlisted him for the 2014 prize with his widely acclaimed *'J'*.

As with his body of work, when Jacobson sets his mind to something it is well worth following him on his intellectual journey. It was such when he addressed the left-wing British group *'Engage'* back in 2007 on the growing specter of academic boycotts against Israeli academics. Yes, it was alive a kicking a decade ago in Britain.

Academic boycotts and intimidation are the antithesis of the meaning and purpose of academic freedoms. Academia should encourage the interchange of ideas. Academia should be an open forum, not a closed society that physically prevents contrary views. It should not be an incubator for dogma, propaganda, incitement, extremism and hatred.

It was this poisoning atmosphere as it was developing on campuses then that compelled Howard Jacobson to share his thoughts with *Engage* in London;

"Defensive academics say it's not about gagging or boycotting Israeli academics. It's about not being prepared to listen to them.

Not listening is a more brutal act than silence. It's a brutal act that you perform on yourself, knowingly, purposefully, and on principle.

Not to listen is to wage war on your own faculties. To deny yourself, if you are a reasoning person, the tools with which you reason.

Once you announce to the world that you stop listening is the moment you announce what you think, and that is the moment when you cease to be a scholar or a teacher.

A university that will not listen causes more damage on itself than to the university that it will not listen to.

It is amazing how certain the boycotters are about absolutely everything. It is this unwavering certitude that is almost religious or ethnic hatred where unreason battens down the mind.

As for the proposition that it's not anti-Semitic to be critical of Israel, like the idea that those that want Israel closed down are being 'critical.'

Critical is a word we associate with measured argument, cool analysis, and fine distinction. Being critical is when you say 'the book works here, doesn't work there, bad plot, poor characterization, liked some parts, hated others.'

What being critical is not is saying, 'this is the most odious book ever written, should never have been published in the first place, must be banned and, in the meantime, should not be read.'

For that, we need another word for 'critical.'

So, when we accuse the boycotters of bigotry, we say they must be fired by an animosity they don't declare and, perhaps, don't even realize they possess.

It's because we cannot understand the inordinacy of their language when they say that Israel is more fascist than the fascists, more Nazi than the Nazis, practicing an apartheid that exceeds the apartheid of South Africa, an Israel that is guilty of every crime against humanity, and doubtless one or two more we haven't yet discovered, torture, assassination, ethnic cleansing, colonization, genocide, massacre, indiscriminate slaughter, and even it can be grudgingly seen to be retaliating it does so 'disproportionately.'

This is no country that ever was outside Hades. So let them tell us if Jew hating is not at the heart of it, what is?

In what furnace of the mind is this nation, evil beyond all others, forged? And why, in its pitiless unheeding malevolence does it so closely resemble the closed cosmos of the pariah Jew as it appears to the medieval imagination?

Let them not be anti-Semites. Let them love the individual Jew as much as they hate the Jewish conglomeration. That does not absolve them of every crime. You can be a bad man and not hate Jews. You can be a disgrace to the profession of teaching and not hate Jews.

We need a language free of issues of religion and ethnicity to describe the intellectual crime, quite simply, of picking on one nation state and loathing it above all others, and against all reason, of simplifying history to fit a narrative that flatters your ideology of victim and oppressor, of imposing a Manichean view of good and evil on events that defy such categorization and can only be inflamed by it, and of shutting down every ingress of the intelligence through which the

arguments of those who think differently to you, or simply want to converse with you about it, can be heard.

In the end, it is not about Israel or Jews at all. It is about the way we practice thought. It is about the idea we have of a university and what constitutes the free play of ideas. It is about the closing of the academic mind.

The boycott is their Dunciad. 'Thy hand great dullness let the curtain fall, and let universal darkness cover all!'"

Howard Jacobson, prompted by the closing of the academic mind and the Jewish condition, has applied his great intellect to a rarely spoken common sense and clarity. It is amazing to me that he has not been urged to enter the once hallowed halls of academia to cast his shining light in their dark corners.

MATTI FRIEDMAN.

This was his address to the BICOM Conference in London.

"I have been writing from and about Israel for most of the past 20 years, since I moved there from Toronto at age 17. During the five and a half years I spent as part of the international press corps as a reporter for the American news agency The Associated Press (AP), between 2006 and 2011, I gradually began to be aware of certain malfunctions in the coverage of the Israel story – recurring omissions, recurring inflations, decisions made according to considerations that were not journalistic but political, all in the context of a story staffed and reported more than any other international story on earth. When I worked in the AP's Jerusalem bureau, the Israel story was covered by more AP news staff than China, or India, or all of the 50-odd countries of sub-Saharan Africa combined. This is representative of the industry as a whole.

In early 2009, to give one fairly routine example of an editorial decision of the kind I mean, I was instructed by my superiors to report a second-hand story taken from an Israeli newspaper about offensive t-shirts supposedly worn by Israeli soldiers. We had no confirmation of our own of the story's veracity, and one doesn't see much coverage of things US Marines or British infantrymen have tattooed on their chests or arms. And yet t-shirts worn by Israeli soldiers were newsworthy in the eyes of one of the world's most powerful news organizations. This was because we sought to hint or say outright that Israeli soldiers were war criminals, and every detail supporting that portrayal was to be seized upon. Much of the international press corps covered the t-shirt story. At around the same time, several Israeli soldiers were quoted anonymously in a school newsletter speaking of abuses they had supposedly witnessed while fighting in Gaza; we wrote no fewer than three separate stories about this, although the use of sources whose identity isn't known to reporters is banned for good reason by the AP's own in-house rules. This story, too, was very much one that we wanted to tell. By the time the soldiers came forward to say they hadn't actually witnessed the events they supposedly described, and were trying to make a point to young students about the horrors and moral challenges of warfare, it was, of course, too late.

Also in those same months, in early 2009, two reporters in our bureau obtained details of a peace offer made by the Israeli Prime Minister, Ehud Olmert, to the Palestinians several months before, and deemed by the Palestinians to be insufficient.
The offer proposed a Palestinian state in the West Bank and Gaza with a capital in a shared Jerusalem.
This should have been one of the year's biggest stories. But an Israeli peace offer and its rejection by the Palestinians didn't suit *our* story. The bureau chief ordered both reporters to ignore the Olmert offer, and they did, despite a furious protest from one of them, who later termed this decision *"The biggest fiasco I've seen in 50 years of journalism."* But it was very much in keeping not only with the practice at the AP, but in the press corps in general. A soldier's vile t-shirts were worth a story. Anonymous and unverifiable testimonies of abuses were worth three. A peace proposal from the Israeli prime minister to the Palestinian president was not to be reported at all.

Vandalism of Palestinian property is a story. Neo-Nazi rallies at Palestinian universities or in Palestinian cities are not – I saw images of such rallies suppressed on more than one occasion. Jewish hatred of Arabs is a story. Arab hatred of Jews is not. Our policy, for example, was not to mention the assertion in the Hamas founding charter that Jews were responsible for engineering both world wars and the Russian and French revolutions, despite the obvious insight this provides into the thinking of one of the most influential actors in the conflict.

A hundred houses in a West Bank settlement are a story. A hundred rockets smuggled into Gaza are not. The Hamas military build-up amid and under the civilian population of Gaza is not a story. But Israeli military action responding to that threat - that is a story as we all saw in 2014. Israel's responsibility for the death of civilians as a result – that's a story. Hamas's responsibility for those deaths is not. Any reporter from the international press corps in Israel, whether he or she works for the AP, Reuters, CNN, the BBC, or elsewhere, will recognize the examples I've cited here of what is newsworthy and what is not as standard operating procedure.

In my time in the press corps I saw, from the inside, how Israel's flaws were dissected and magnified, while the flaws of its enemies were purposely erased. I saw how the threats facing Israel were disregarded or even mocked as figments of the Israeli imagination, even as these threats repeatedly materialized. I saw how a fictional image of Israel and of its enemies was manufactured, polished, and propagated to devastating effect by inflating certain details, ignoring others, and presenting the result as an accurate picture of reality.

Lest we think this is something that has never happened before, we might remember Orwell's observation about journalism from the Spanish Civil War: *"Early in life,"* he wrote, *"I had noticed that no event is ever correctly reported in a newspaper, but in Spain, for the first time, I saw newspaper reports which do not bear any relation to the facts, not even the relationship which is implied in an ordinary lie. I saw, in fact, history being written not in terms of what had happened but of what ought to have happened according to various 'party lines.'"* That was in 1942.

Over time, I came to understand that the malfunctions I was witnessing, and in which I was playing a part, were not limited to the AP. I saw that they were rather part of a broader problem in the way the press functioned, and in how it saw its job.

The international press in Israel had become less an observer of the conflict than a player in it. It had moved away from careful explanation and toward a kind of political character assassination on behalf of the side it identified as being right. It valued a kind of ideological uniformity from which you were not allowed to stray. So having begun with limited criticism of certain editorial decisions, I now found myself with a broad critique of the press.

Eventually, however, I realized that even the press wasn't the whole story. The press was playing a key role in an intellectual phenomenon taking root in the West, but it wasn't the cause, or not the only cause – it was both blown on a certain course by the prevailing ideological winds, and causing those winds to blow with greater force. Many journalists would like you to believe that the news is created by a kind of algorithm – that it's a mechanical, even scientific, process in which events are inserted, processed, and presented. But of course the news is an imperfect and entirely human affair, the result of interactions between sources, reporters, and editors, all of whom bear the baggage of their background and who reflect, as we all do to some extent, the prejudices of their peers.

In the aftermath of last summer's Gaza war, and in light of events in Europe in recent months, it should be clear that something deep and toxic is going on. Understanding what that is, it seems to me, will help us understand something important not only about journalism but about the Western mind and the way it sees the world.

What presents itself as political criticism, as analysis, or as journalism, is coming to sound more and more like a new version of a much older complaint — that Jews are troublemakers, a negative force in world events, and that if these people, as a collective, could somehow be made to vanish, we would all be better off. This is, or should be, a cause for alarm, and not only among people sympathetic to Israel or concerned with Jewish affairs. What is in play right now has less to do with the world of politics than with the worlds of psychology and religion, and less to do with Israel than with those condemning Israel.

The occupation of the West Bank, with which I opened, would seem to be at the heart of the story, the root cause, as it were, of the conflict portrayed as the most important on earth. A few words, then, about this occupation.

The occupation was created in the 1967 Mideast War. The occupation is not the conflict, which of course predates the occupation. It is a symptom of the conflict, a conflict that would remain even if the symptom were somehow solved. If we look at the West Bank, the only Palestinian area currently occupied by Israel, and if we include Jerusalem, we see that the conflict in these areas claimed 60 lives last year — Palestinian and Israeli.

An end to this occupation would free Palestinians from Israeli rule, and free Israelis from ruling people who do not wish to be ruled. Observers of the Middle East in 2015 understand, too, that an end to the occupation will create a power vacuum that will be filled, as all power vacuums in the region have been, not by the forces of democracy and modernity, which in our region range from weak to negligible, but by the powerful and ruthless, by the extremists. This is what we've learned from the unravelling of the Middle East in recent years. This is what happened in Iraq, Syria, Libya, Yemen, and Egypt, and before that in Gaza and southern

Lebanon. My home in Jerusalem is within an easy day's drive of both Aleppo and Baghdad. Creating a new playground for these forces will bring the black-masked soldiers of radical Islam within yards of Israeli homes with mortars, rockets, and tunneling implements. Many thousands will die.

Beyond the obvious threat to Palestinian Christians, women, gays, and liberals, who will be the first to suffer, this threatens to render much or all of Israel unlivable, ending the only safe progressive space in the Middle East, the only secure minority refuge in the Middle East, and the only Jewish country on earth. No international investment or guarantees, no Western-backed government or Western-trained military will be able to keep that from happening, as we have just seen in Iraq. The world will greet this outcome with sincere expressions of sympathy. Only several years ago I, like many on the left, might have dismissed this as an apocalyptic scenario. It isn't. It is the most likely scenario.

People observing this conflict from afar have been led to believe that Israel faces a simple choice between occupation and peace. That choice is fiction. The Palestinian choice, it is said, is between Israeli occupation and an independent democracy. That choice, too, is fiction. Neither side faces a clear choice, or clear outcomes. Here we have a conflict in a region of conflict, with no clear villain, no clear victim, and no clear solution, one of many hundreds or thousands of ethnic, national, and religious disputes on earth.

The only group of people subject to a systematic boycott at present in the Western world is Jews, appearing now under the convenient euphemism 'Israelis.' The only country that has its own 'apartheid week' on campuses is the Jewish country. Protesters have interfered with the unloading of Israeli shipping on the West Coast of the United States, and there are regular calls for a boycott of anything produced in the Jewish state. No similar tactics are currently employed against any other ethnic group or nationality, no matter how egregious the human rights violations attributed to that group's country of origin.

Anyone who questions why this is so will be greeted with shouts of *'the occupation!'*, as if this were explanation enough. It is not. Many who would like to question these phenomena don't dare, for fear that they will somehow be expressing support for this occupation, which has been inflated from a geopolitical dilemma of modest scope by global standards into the world's premier violation of human rights.

The human costs of the Middle Eastern adventures of America and Britain in this century have been far higher, and far harder to explain, than anything Israel has ever done. They have involved occupations, and the violence they unleashed continues as I speak here this evening. No one boycotts American or British professors. Turkey is a democracy, and a NATO member, and yet its occupation of northern Cyprus and long conflict with the stateless Kurds – many of whom see themselves as occupied – are viewed with a yawn; there is no *'Turkish Apartheid Week.'* The world is full of injustice. Billions of people are oppressed. In Congo, five million people are dead. The time has come for everyone to admit that the fashionable disgust for Israel among many in the West is not liberal but is selective, disproportionate, and discriminatory.

There are simply too many voices coming from too many places, expressing themselves in too poisonous a way, for us to conclude that this is a narrow criticism of the occupation. It's time for the people making these charges to look closely at themselves, and for us to look closely at them.

Naming and understanding this sentiment is important, as it is becoming one of the key intellectual trends of our time. We might think of it as the *'Cult of the Occupation.'* This belief system, for that it what it is, uses the occupation as a way of talking about other things.

As usual with Western religions, the center of this one is in the Holy Land. The dogma posits that the occupation is not a conflict like any other, but that it is the very symbol of conflict: that the minute state inhabited by a persecuted minority in the Middle East is in fact a symbol of the ills of the West – colonialism, nationalism, militarism, and racism. In the recent riots in Ferguson, Missouri, for example, a sign hoisted by marchers linked the unrest between African Americans and the police to Israeli rule over Palestinians.

The cult's priesthood can be found among the activists, NGO experts, and ideological journalists who have turned coverage of this conflict into a catalogue of Jewish moral failings, as if Israeli society were different from any other group of people on earth, as if Jews deserve to be mocked for having suffered and failed to be perfect as a result.

Most of my former colleagues in the press corps aren't full-fledged members of this group. They aren't true believers. But boycotts of Israel, and only of Israel, which are one of the cult's most important practices, have significant support in the press, including among editors who were my superiors. Sympathy for Israel's predicament is highly unpopular in the relevant social circles, and is something to be avoided by anyone wishing to be invited to the right dinner parties, or to be promoted. The cult and its belief system are in control of the narrative, just as the popular kids in a school are those who decide what clothes or music are acceptable. In the social milieu of the reporters, NGO workers, and activists, which is the same social world, these are the correct opinions. This guides the coverage. This explains why the events in Gaza this summer were portrayed not as a complicated war like many others fought in this century, but as a massacre of innocents. And it explains much else.

So prevalent has this kind of thinking become that participating in liberal intellectual life in the West increasingly requires you to subscribe at least outwardly to this dogma, particularly if you're a Jew and thus suspected of the wrong sympathies. If you're a Jew from Israel, your participation is increasingly conditional on an abject and public display of self-flagellation. Your participation, indeed, is increasingly unwelcome.

What, exactly, is going on?

Observers of Western history understand that at times of confusion and unhappiness, and of great ideological ferment, negative sentiment tends to coagulate around Jews. Discussions of the great topics of the time often end up as discussions about Jews.

In the late 1800s, for example, French society was riven by the clash between the old France of the church and army, and the new France of liberalism and the rule of law. The French were preoccupied with the question of who is French, and who is not. They were smarting from their military humiliation by the Prussians. All of this sentiment erupted around the figure of a Jew, Alfred Dreyfus, accused of betraying France as a spy for Germany. His accusers knew he was innocent, but that didn't matter; he was a symbol of everything they wanted to condemn.

To give another example: Germans in the 1920s and 1930s were preoccupied with their humiliation in the Great War. This became a discussion of Jewish traitors who had stabbed Germany in the back. Germans were preoccupied as well with the woes of their economy – this became a discussion of Jewish wealth, and Jewish bankers.

In the years of the rise of communism and the Cold War, communists concerned with their ideological opponents talked about Jewish capitalists and cosmopolitans, or Jewish doctors plotting against the state. At the very same time, in capitalist societies threatened by communism, people condemned Jewish Bolsheviks.

This is the face of this recurring obsession. As the journalist Charles Maurras wrote, approvingly, in 1911: *"Everything seems impossible, or frighteningly difficult, without the providential arrival of anti-Semitism, through which all things fall into place and are simplified."*

The West today is preoccupied with a feeling of guilt about the use of power. That's why the Jews, in their state, are now held up in the press and elsewhere as the prime example of the abuse of power. That's why for so many the global villain, as portrayed in newspapers and on TV, is none other than the Jewish soldier, or the Jewish settler. This is not because the Jewish settler or soldier is responsible for more harm than anyone else on earth – no sane person would make that claim. It is rather because these are the heirs to the Jewish banker or Jewish commissar of the past. It is because when moral failure raises its head in the Western imagination, the head tends to wear a skullcap.

One would expect the growing scale and complexity of the conflict in the Middle East over the past decade to have eclipsed the fixation on Israel in the eyes of the press and other observers. Israel is, after all, a sideshow: The death toll in Syria in less than four years far exceeds the toll in the Israel-Arab conflict in a century. The annual death toll in the West Bank and Jerusalem is a morning in Iraq.

And yet it is precisely in these years that the obsession has grown worse.

This makes little sense, unless we understand that people aren't fixated on Israel despite everything else going on – but rather because of everything else going on. As Maurras wrote, when you use the Jew as the symbol of what is wrong, *"all things fall into place and are simplified."*

The last few decades have brought the West into conflict with the Islamic world. Terrorists have attacked New York, Washington, London, Madrid, and now Paris. America and Britain caused the unravelling of Iraq, and hundreds of thousands of people are dead there. Afghanistan was occupied and thousands of Western soldiers killed, along with countless civilians – but the Taliban are alive and well, undeterred. Gaddafi was removed, and Libya is no better off. All of this is confusing and discouraging. It causes people to search for answers and explanations, and these are hard to come by. It is in this context that the *'Cult of the*

Occupation' has caught on. The idea is that the problems in the Middle East have something to do with Jewish arrogance and perfidy, that the sins of one's own country can be projected upon the Western world's old blank screen. This is the idea increasingly reflected on campuses, in labor unions, and in the media fixation on Israel. It's a projection, one whose chief instrument is the press.

As one BBC reporter informed a Jewish interviewee on camera several weeks ago, after a Muslim terrorist murdered four Jewish shoppers at a Paris supermarket, *"Many critics of Israel's policy would suggest that the Palestinians suffered hugely at Jewish hands as well."*

Everything, that is, can be linked to the occupation, and Jews can be blamed even for the attacks against them. This isn't the voice of the perpetrators, but of the enablers. The voice of the enablers is less honest than that of the perpetrators, and more dangerous for being disguised in respectable English. This voice is confident and growing in volume. This is why the year 2015 found many Jews in Western Europe eyeing their suitcases again.

The Jews of the Middle East are outnumbered by the Arabs of the Middle East 60 to one, and by the world's Muslims 200 to one. Half of the Jews in Israel are there because their families were forced from their homes in the 20th century, not by Christians in Europe but by Muslims in the Middle East.

Israel currently has Hezbollah on its northern border, Al-Qaeda on its north-eastern and southern borders, and Hamas in Gaza. None of these groups seek an end to the occupation, but rather openly wish to destroy Israel. But it is naïve to point out these facts. The facts don't matter: We are in the world of symbols. In this world, Israel has become a symbol of what is wrong – not Hamas, not Hezbollah, not Great Britain, not America, not Russia.

I believe it's important to recognize the pathologies at play in order to make sense of things. In this context it's worth pointing out that I'm hardly the first to identify a problem – Jewish communities like this one, and particularly organizations like BICOM, identified a problem long ago, and have been expending immense efforts to correct it. I wish this wasn't necessary, and it shouldn't be necessary, but it undoubtedly is necessary, and becoming more so, and I have great respect for these efforts. Many people, particularly young people, are having trouble maintaining their balance amid this ideological onslaught, which is successfully disguised as journalism or analysis, and is phrased in the language of progressive politics. I would like to help them keep their bearings.

I don't believe, however, that anyone should make a feeling of persecution the center of their identity, of their Judaism, or of their relationship with Israel. The obsession is a fact, but it isn't a new fact, and it shouldn't immobilize us in anger, or force us into a defensive crouch. It shouldn't make us less willing to seek to improve our situation, to behave with compassion to our neighbors, or to continue building the model society that Israel's founders had in mind.

I was in Tel Aviv not long ago, on Rothschild Boulevard. The city was humming with life. Signs of prosperity were everywhere, in the renovated Bauhaus buildings, in the clothes, the stores. I watched the people go by: kids with old bikes and tattoos, businesspeople, men with women, women with women, men with men, all speaking the language of the Bible and Jewish prayer. The summer's Hamas rockets were already a memory, just a few months old but subsumed in the frantic, irrepressible life of the country. There were cranes everywhere, raising new buildings. There were schoolchildren with oversized knapsacks, and parents with strollers. I heard Arabic, Russian, and French, and the country went about its business with a potent cheer and determination that you miss if all you see are threats and hatred. There have always been threats and hatred, and it has never stopped us. We have enemies, and we have friends. The dogs bark, as the saying goes, and the convoy rolls by.

One of the questions presented to us by the wars of the modern age is what now constitutes victory. In the 21st century, when a battlefield is no longer conquered or lost, when land isn't changing hands and no one ever surrenders, what does it mean to win?

The answer is that victory is no longer determined on the battlefield. It's determined in the center, in the society itself. Who has built a better society? Who has provided better lives for people? Where is there the most optimism? Where can the happiest people be found? One report on world happiness ranked Israel as the 11th happiest country on earth. The UK was 22nd.

Israel's intellectual opponents can rant about the moral failings of the Jews, obscuring their obsession in whatever sophisticated way they choose. The gunmen of Hamas and their allies can stand on heaps of rubble and declare victory. They can fire rockets, and shoot up supermarkets. But if you look at Tel Aviv, or at any thriving neighborhood in Jerusalem, Netanya, Rishon LeZion, or Haifa, you understand that this is victory. This is where we've won, and where we win every day."

BASSAM EID. A Palestinian human rights advocate that opposes BDS and boycotts.

Bassam Eid is a Palestinian human rights activist. He created Palestinian human rights Monitoring Group that focuses on human rights violations by and corruption in the Palestinian Authority. No other 'human rights' organization focus on citizen abuses at the hands of the Palestinian leadership both in Ramallah and in Gaza. He was jailed by the Palestinian Authority for his work.

"There are many human rights organizations in Israel whereas there is hardly any in the Palestinian-controlled areas that monitor its actions in this regard," Eid says.

Eid's organization received significant funding from European governments and managed to employ researchers who operated in the West Bank and the Gaza Strip. Five years ago, however, things changed and funding came to an end.

Why would the Europeans decide to stop funding a human rights organization that reports of crimes and abuses committed by the Palestinian leadership against their own people?

"I think it happened because the European policy in recent years has been to come down hard on Israel and not the Palestinian leadership," Bassam Eid said.

"They view Israel as the main obstacle to the peace process and want to support the Palestinian Authority. One of the ways to show this support is to stop funding organizations that are critical of the Palestinian Authority."

In an interview with YNetNews, Eid said, *"I'm opposed to the boycott because it only ends up harming the Palestinians themselves. Take, for example, the SodaStream plant in Mishor Adumim that is now moving some of its operations to Be'er Sheva. I've met with Palestinians who worked at the factory and were fired because of the move. They told me they were earning an average salary of five thousand shekels a month there and, today, they are being offered salaries of only one thousand four hundred shekels in the Palestinian Authority.*

People there are now in deep debt because they have taken on long-term commitments based on the understanding that their work at the plant would continue, but reality slapped them in the face because of the pressure created by the BDS movement. Today, they are running between the courts and the bailiff office and is anyone taking any notice of them? Do you think the boycott movement cares about them at all?"

For his outspoken truth about what is going on within Palestinian society Eid was threatened and prevented from speaking at the University of Johannesburg by BDS protesters in March 2015.

About the Palestinian Authority, Eid told Rebel Media, *"The Palestinian Authority is living in one valley and the Palestinian people are living in another valley. There is no communication between the two."*

"Almost not one Palestinian has benefited from the money coming from abroad to the Palestinian Authority. As a society we talk a lot about the corruption of the Authority. Unfortunately, the international community still has blind eyes about this corruption."

"Nobody is talking about the foundation of a Palestinian state. Forget any reconciliation or unity between Fatah and Hamas. Although the international community is demanding two states for two people, the Palestinians are calling for three states for two people. Hamas is fighting for its own interest in Gaza while Fatah is fighting for its own interest in Ramallah, and Israel."

On the other Arab states, Eid says, *"I'm not sure that there is even one Arab state that is in favor of a Palestinian state, despite what they say. If you take the Palestinian case from 1948 until 1967, the West Bank and east Jerusalem was under the control of the Jordanians and the Gaza Strip was under Egyptian control. Did Jordan or Egypt between 1948 and 1967 ever try to create a Palestinian state? I am not sure the Arabs are interested in the foundation of a Palestinian state and most of the Arab countries are stuck in their own mud."*

To Israel, he says, *"You must remember that your country is still feeding 1,800,000 Palestinian in the Gaza Strip. The State of Israel is supplying food, medicine and fuel while 22 Arab do nothing and watch Israeli trucks bring supplies into Gaza.*

You are still feeding us Palestinians and, thanks to you, we are surviving."

CAROLINE GLICK.

"Why should Jews be allowed to live in London, in Germany, live in San Francisco, but not allowed to live in Judea and Samaria, and in Jerusalem? Why? Where did this come from?

They want to talk so much about Palestinian rights, let's just talk about Jewish rights for a second. You are saying that you support a Palestinian state that is going to be inherently bigoted and that Jews aren't allowed to live there, that they all have to be ethnically cleansed, before these people even deign to accept sovereignty. What sort of state do you want to establish? What kind of nonsense is this? This is a racket.

Jews don't have civil rights? We are not allowed to live where ever we have property rights to build just because we're Jewish? And this is a moral argument? This is a reasonable argument? This is establishing what exactly? A state based upon ethnic purity? This is where we have come to in 2015 in the Western world? Where are the liberal values that are being advanced by this cause of a Jew-free Palestine?

Can somebody explain this to me because I don't understand it?"

You want to know what we're really talking about here when we talk about throwing all these Jews off the land that we bought, that belongs to us? We are talking about trying to find common ground with terrorist organizations that are mandated to enact a genocide of the Jewish People. Just read the Hamas Charter. Just read what they say. They call not only for the annihilation and obliteration, in their words, of the Jewish state, but they call for the annihilation of world Jewry. And to try to find common ground with these murderers, or with Holocaust deniers like PLO chief Mahmoud Abbbas.

PAT CONDELL.

I love Pat Condell. You can find his terrific video monologues on YouTube.

Condell cuts through the bull with his acerbic wit. He exposes the floundering of progressive/regressive politics with well-chosen irony. He is doubly scathing of the enemies that oppose our way of life and wish to destroy it. In short, he speaks decisively for those of us who care.

"It isn't always easy to change your mind especially when your opinions are based on emotions and not facts, but I'm encouraged to see that some people are beginning to change their mind about despite the relentless anti-Israel coverage we're constantly forced-fed by the Western media. Because, when people take the trouble to look at the facts, they quickly realize that the Palestinian cause is insultingly bogus, that the terrorist Palestinian leadership is playing the free world like a Stradivarius and that the whole problem could be solved peacefully and prosperously for everyone involved tomorrow if only they would stop murdering people and let it happen.

People also realize when they look at the facts that for all the talk of an apartheid state in Israel the only apartheid you'll find in the Middle East is in Arab countries who won't allow their Palestinians to integrate, denying them the most basic of human rights and condemning them to generations of misery and resentment because they need the refugee camps to remain permanently festering like open sores to gain sympathy from the gullible West and to con millions of good hearted people here into supporting their religious war of hatred against Jews, all Jews. Indeed the Hamas Charter specifically calls for the killing of all Jews, just in case anyone was in any doubt.

However, although the tide of truth is beginning to turn, many people are still very critical of Israel's failure to abide by United Nations resolutions, especially to do with human rights. And yet, on the surface, that seems a legitimate concern, assuming of course that a UN resolution is worth the paper it's written on. Let's pretend for the moment that it is, just for fun.

That's a real puzzle, isn't it? Why would the Israelis ignore dozens of resolutions forced through by a cartel of anti-Semitic, bronze-age barbarians who would destroy their country and everyone in it, including women and children given half the chance? Beat's me. I guess they must be fascists.

If you're one of the people who still think like this let me try and explain to you why they do it, in case you are too stubborn or too dense to figure it out for yourself.

The United Nations as it stands today is an embarrassing disgrace and an insult to humanity. Whatever moral authority it may once have had has been squandered. Its political corruption is matched only by its incompetence. Just ask the people of Syria.

I wouldn't trust the United Nations to run a lemonade stand without thousands of people being needlessly killed.

Among its many failings the United Nations encourages Islamic religious hatred and racism to dress itself up in the language of human rights, repeatedly allowing its Human Rights Council to be steamrollered in this regard by a cartel of fifty seven mainly dictatorships and theocracies that is known as the Organization of Islamic something or other. I don't really care what they call themselves, it's enough to know what they are and that's brutal, barbaric Islamic hell holes that nobody in their right mind would choose to live in and whose own human rights records are not only worse than Israel's but immeasurably worse. Countries like Iran where they execute children, Sudan where they practice slavery and casual genocide, Pakistan which is supposed to be democracy but which is actually a dictatorship of religious ignorance, violence and fear and where, every year, a thousand women are murdered by members of their own family. And, of course, Saudi Arabia, the black hole of Islamic barbarism, the world's leading source of terrorist funding and the absolute moral anus of the universe.

These are some of the countries behind the blizzard of resolutions directed at Israel. Countries, that belong on the high moral ground the way that a rattlesnake belongs in a lunchbox. Countries united by a virulent hatred of Jews for being Jews. These are the loudest voices at the United Nations. So, of course, the Israelis ignore them. It would be suicidal not to.

When it comes to Israel, the United Nations is a rooked court with a jury full of hanging judges, and it doesn't get more corrupt than that. Frankly, I'm baffled why the Americans still tolerate this disgusting travesty on their soil and pay all its bills. They should kick it out of the country and tell it to relocate to Tehran or Islamabad where the Organization of Islamic fascists can go ahead and pass all the fancy resolutions they like, all written out in the most beautiful Arabic and then promptly shove them where the sun don't shine.

Attacking Israel over and over, while ignoring the real human rights violators, not only the Islamic barbarians but the North Koreas and the Burmas of this world, the United Nations has shown itself to be nakedly partisan and to be effectively an enemy of Israel.

As I see it, unless you're an idiot or a Western liberal you don't take orders from your enemies."

DEBATING AGAINST BDS AT OXFORD – AND WINNING.

Alan Dershowitz exposes the moral weakness of the BDS movement.

When I was invited to debate in favor of the motion *"Is BDS Wrong?"* at the Oxford Union, I fully expected to lose the vote of the 250 or so students and faculty who are members of the oldest debating society in the world.

"Israel always loses at Oxford," I was warned by colleagues who had debated other Israel-related issues. Nonetheless I decided to participate, hoping to change some minds.

I proposed as my opponent Omar Barghouti, the Qatari-born, Israeli-educated, co-founder and spokesperson of the BDS movement, but he refused to debate me. The Union then selected Noura Erekat, a Palestinian-American human rights attorney, who has been a vocal supporter of BDS.

When she backed out at the last minute, I began to get suspicious: was the BDS movement boycotting me? After all, BDS advocates have called for *"common sense"* academic boycotts against individuals who they feel are too vocal in their support for Israel, in addition to a blanket boycott of all Israeli academic institutions. After speaking with the organizers of the debate at Oxford, I continue to believe that I was in fact being boycotted.

The Union then selected Peter Tatchell, a distinguished and popular British human rights activist who has participated in 30 Union debates, most of which he has won. I knew I was in for a difficult time, especially when the audience applauded his points more loudly than mine and when many of the questions seemed hostile toward Israel, though polite.

Mr. Tatchell's main argument was that BDS was a nonviolent form of protest against Israel's occupation and settlement policies that mirrored the boycott movement against apartheid South Africa, and followed the principles of Mahatma Gandhi and Martin Luther King. He was articulate in arguing that boycott tactics generally were a nonviolent alternative to war and terrorism.

The force of his argument was somewhat weakened by the recent spate of terrorist knife attacks by Palestinians against Israelis, which leaders of the BDS movement, such as Barghouti, have justified as resistance to the *"decades-old regime of occupation."*

I argued that BDS was not an alternative to war but rather an alternative to peaceful negotiations by the Palestinian leadership. This is because the BDS movement is firmly opposed to the two-state solution. Barghouti confirmed as much when he said *"definitely, most definitely, we oppose a Jewish state in any part of Palestine."* Thus, the BDS movement makes it more difficult for the Palestinian leadership to accept the kind of painful compromises that both sides must agree to if there is to be a negotiated resolution.

Together with other efforts to delegitimize and isolate Israel, BDS also sends a false message to the Palestinian street: namely, that international economic and political pressure can force Israel to capitulate to all Palestinian demands, without any compromise on territorial issues. This disincentives the Palestinian leadership from accepting Prime Minister Benjamin Netanyahu's offer to begin immediate negotiations with no preconditions.

Such discussions are particularly important now, to halt the gruesome cycle of violence that has intensified in recent weeks. Both sides must return to the negotiations table, and both must be willing to make concessions. For the Israelis this means rolling back settlements, and granting greater autonomy to the West Bank; for the Palestinian Authority, it means renouncing violence against Israeli civilians, disavowing Hamas and other terrorist organizations, and accepting the need for territorial compromise with land swaps.

BDS opposes any effort at negotiation that isn't premised on the recognition that Israel is an apartheid state.

Indeed, many of its leaders refuse to recognize the right of Israel to exist as a nation-state for the Jewish people. In so doing, they are empowering radicals on both sides of the issue who have no desire to see a peaceful resolution to the conflict.

Many liberal activists such as Mr. Tatchell – whose advocacy on behalf of LGBT rights I greatly admire – have made common cause with BDS, hoping to pressure Israel to end the occupation, and afford greater self-determination to Palestinians in the West Bank.

They seem to believe that a movement advocating nonviolent tactics is necessarily the best way to achieve a lasting peace. But BDS is radically opposed to any negotiated settlement, and has increasingly begun to recruit bigots of all stripes who feel comfortable with the language used by its leaders, such Mr. Barghouti.

Mr. Tatchell and many pro-BDS academics also feel that Israel has committed human rights violations both in the occupation of the West Bank, and in its prosecution of the armed conflicts in Gaza. During the course of the debate I issued the following challenge to the audience and to my opponent: name a single country in the history of the world, faced with threats comparable to those faced by Israel that has a better record of human rights, compliance with the rule of law and seeking to minimize civilian casualties.

I invited audience members to shout out the name of a country. Complete silence. Finally someone shouted "Iceland," and everyone laughed. When the best is treated as the worst, in the way the BDS movement singles out Israel for accusation, the finger of blame must be pointed at the accusers rather than the accused. In the end, the case against BDS won not because of the comparative skill of the debaters but because I was able to expose the moral weakness of the BDS movement itself.

The author is the Felix Frankfurter Emeritus Professor at Harvard Law School and the author of two new books: The Case against the Iran Deal: How Can We Now Stop Iran from Getting Nukes? Available on Kindle and other eBook sites, and Abraham: The World's First (But Certainly Not Last) Jewish Lawyer, available on Amazon and in bookstores.

WHO IS A GREATER THREAT TO PEACE – HAMAS, OR ISRAEL?

Denis Prager is a radio show host and President of the Prager University. He was invited to debate this proposition at the Oxford Union.

Here are his words;

"Two things I found remarkable when I was first invited (to speak). One is I actually did not believe the proposition. It was that *"This house believes that Hamas is a greater threat to peace than Israel, "*and I give you my word of honor that I actually called Oxford, I went online. I couldn't believe this was an actual proposition. You mean that that's debatable? I actually thought that pro-Israel forces at Oxford had somehow pushed this into the line-up as we say in America when you push for a line-up for your players on your team.

I was stunned.

The other was when I realized *'By God! They actually they are serious! This must be an academic institution'*. As Orwell once said, *'some things are so foolish only an intellectual can believe them'* and I realized, *'OK. This is it. This is a Western world tragedy, the amount of nonsense that is actually believed in academia.'* And so this is a debatable proposition at such an illustrious institution? That being said, as I will point out over and over just appealing to your common sense, you need to know nothing about the Middle East to know how absurd the proposition is. It's of course valid, but that is debatable as an absurdity.

My other thing is my biography. I must say I have been called many things, even controversial, but of my long resume just to be described as controversial may I say to you to the millions of people I broadcast to every day I am not controversial whatsoever. So clearly those that invited me find it controversial.

Let me just give you an analogy. I didn't check, I should have, but if in the 1930s there had been a debate at this auspicious place over the following proposition, *'That Great Britain is a greater threat to peace than Nazi Germany, or is Nazi Germany a greater threat to peace than Great Britain?'*

Was there a debate in the 1930s? That is a perfect analogy to what we are debating tonight. Nazi Germany was to Britain what Hamas is to Israel. Whether you agree with Israeli policies or not, and I don't agree with all Israeli policies, it is irrelevant. The question is, is that analogy fair?

So let me ask you a question. Who is the greater threat to peace in Syria - ISIS, or Israel? Who is the greater threat to peace in Lebanon – Hezbollah, or Israel? Who is the greater threat to peace in Egypt – the Muslim Brotherhood, or Israel? Do you understand? In every case everyone in this room would acknowledge that ISIS is a greater threat to peace in Syria, that Hezbollah is a greater threat to peace in Lebanon, that the Muslim

Brotherhood is a greater threat to peace in Egypt. All of a sudden we change the entire scenario because it is now Hamas instead of Hezbollah, or ISIS, or the Muslim Brotherhood?

On this issue, just to appeal to your common sense, in modern history every war has been between a free state and a police state or between two police states. I cannot think of a 20th Century example of any other. And the same holds true here. You have the police state of Hamas – if you differ with Hamas they kill you. Where in the world today, other than Israel, does anyone ever argue that the free state doesn't want peace and the police state wants peace? There is no other example on earth. There is no other example on earth of a country targeted for extinction. None! There are two hundred and twenty countries in this world. Only Israel is targeted for extinction. And we have a debate on whether the state targeted for extinction is the barrier to peace? That is quite a leap of faith.

In the age of beheadings, as you have tragically experienced here in the UK, we have a debate? Hamas is a kindred spirit to ISIS and Hezbollah and Bobo Haram. What do you think? That they are an exception? All of those are monstrous, but Hamas, they're a terrific bunch who really want peace. If it only weren't for settlements! There were no settlements prior to 1967. Why wasn't there peace? Israel would dismantle the settlements in a moment because the Israeli people are much more interested in sending their kids to college, and having a peaceful life, and in making a good living, and inventing more medical and technological devices, than they are in fighting wars.

This would be the first free state in history to prefer war to peace. It is highly, highly, unlikely.

The Hamas Covenant says *'Israel will exist until Islam will obliterate it, just as it obliterated others before it. The Islamic Resistance Movement is a distinguished Palestinian movement whose allegiance is to Allah and whose way of life is Islam.* ' It ascribes to battle of Allah over every inch of Palestine. That's what Hamas is devoted to."

There was interference from a female member of the opposing speakers.

"All of the organizations you are citing as a threat to peace just happen to be Arab and/or Muslim. Could you explain to me why you think that might be the case that you only refer to these organizations as a threat to peace?"

This question received applause from the audience. Prager answered;

"Obviously those of you who applauded perceived the profundity of the question that I didn't. I don't quite understand. They are all threats to peace. That is correct. Why did I only pick on Arab Muslims? I said Boko Haram. They are not Arab Muslims. The only beheadings we've seen to date, to the best of my knowledge, have either been by Arabs or Muslims."

"Why do you think that is?" the lady challenged.

"Why do I think that is? Sad to say, it was answered by Arab intellectuals at the United Nations because the Arab world is in a benighted place at this time. The status of Arab women is particularly low. In ten years, the Arab world translates fewer books than Greece does in one year. There is no interest in the foreign world. It is a benighted world, the Arab world. This is a tragedy. It is not anti-Arab. If you love Arabs you have to understand how low the moral level of the Arab world at this point is. And that has nothing to do with individual Arabs that may be saintly, but that is the dominant moral state. You are taught that you cannot judge civilization on the same moral level. That is to give up on hope for humanity to claim there is no civilization that lets us produce something better. That is the tragic reason. They are not beheading people in

Western civilization. They are in the Arab and Muslim world, and not entirely in the Arab and Muslim world.

My second part is the answer the question, why is something so obvious as Israel wants peace and that Hamas wants to destroy Israel being debated at one of the world's most illustrious academic institutes. I have two answers.

One is that there has been a broken moral compass in the intellectual world in the West for perhaps the last eighty or hundred years. I will give you an example. I studied at Columbia University at the School of International Affairs. I was taught by brilliant professors that the United States and the Soviet Union were the same moral equivalents. It was Capitalism versus Communism. Two economic theories, that's all. Neither was better than the other. You may not recall, because many of you weren't born, but Ronald Reagan, the President of the United States, called the Soviet Union *'an evil empire.'* He was lambasted. He was declared by Columbia and Harvard and Yale and Princeton and the New York Times as a fool for having the temerity to make a moral statement about the Soviet Union, a place that had created the Gulag Archipelago that had killed forty million of its own people, not to mention a genocide in the Ukraine. That is what has taken over in Western universities. A broken moral compass that fools call good evil, and evil good. I went through this, and many of you are going through this, and this evening is just one example.

Finally, the media. The media gives you a jaundiced view of the world. Gaza started as war to kill as many Israelis as possible, and all you see on the BBC, Sky News and CNN is dead Gazans. That's all you see. I shudder to think if, in World War Two, they made the same media coverage. You would have seen far more dead German civilians that dead British civilians. But it takes a very frail moral mind to believe that you determine right from wrong by the number of dead. That's what we are told. Look at how many Gazans were killed and how few Israelis. Well look at how few Brits were killed and how many more Germans were. Does that make the Germans right in World War Two? That's the facile moral case that pervades our world.

So I end with this. It would be a tragedy if it were known that the Oxford Union actually declared that Israel, and not Hamas, is the greater threat to peace. Outside the world of academia it's pretty clear.

It's got to be pretty clear here too.

RANDOM THOUGHTS ON A WORLD GONE MAD.

SOUTH AFRICA- THE LEADING HUB OF BDS.

BDS should be taken lightly. As I mentioned earlier, they tend to talk in slogans. Anyone with a smattering of knowledge, history and facts can shoot them down with ease.

The strange thing is that many people take them seriously and adopt their nonsense. When this happens at government level it's time to get our hands dirty sifting through the stench of BDS garbage to expose the truth.

A good place to start is in South Africa, one of the major trash cans of BDS sewage. Globally, there are a few depositories of BDS rubbish and South Africa is one.

This country is in political meltdown since the days of Nelson Mandela though proud Springboks will deny this even as their country limps from one scandal to another.

Mandela's legacy has been corrupted by the rot within his ANC party from local level all the way up to President Jacob Zuma.

When the allegations of payments by Hitachi amounting to tens of millions of dollars to an ANC entity to build two power plants, broke an opposition leader, Mmusi Maimane, accused ANC of *"systematic corruption endemic within ANC."*

The feeble push-back by ANC amounted to a representative saying that *"the money was never given by Hitachi to ANC. It was given to a company linked with the ANC."*

What he failed to disclose that people bonded to both entities were caught with their fingers in the till.

President Zuma has shrugged off multiple scandals that would have downed any leader in a democratic society. These scandals include taking more than seven hundred bribes from arms dealers, admitting fathering a child out of wedlock with a friend's daughter, and squandering taxpayers' money to the tune of almost $18 million on upgrades to his private home.

His resilience to scandals stems from his nepotism. He has packed key posts with loyalists, and paid off the poor population with extended welfare grants that leave the South African economy groaning.

As Pretoria University political lecturer, Mzukisi Qobo, put it, *"He is untouchable. Those who have positions in government will remain silent because they will not want to lose the patronage they have. It is a vain hope to think that any leader or member of the ANC will stand up to him and not suffer consequences."*

Opposition politicians have been attacked and people have been intimidated by member of the powerful ANC so regularly that it has become part of the political climate in South Africa.

Political assassinations have been common in post-Apartheid South Africa. This has been particularly rife within the ANC where rivals have been competing for positions of influence and power.

The party of Mandela has seemingly become the party of Guevara and Castro. Its politics, on a number of levels, equate to those of Cuba and the Israel-Palestinian issue is one.

ANC and BDS are, today, linked at the hip. Both see themselves as revolutionary lefties championing the downtrodden against imperialist colonialist oppressors. This is their worldview as applied to Israel.

Following this misplaced logic, Arabs become the new Blacks of the Middle East and Israeli Jews become the new white regime. Such a convenient colloquialism allows them to cast Israel as an apartheid state while equating Palestinian terrorism to the ANC fight against white rule.

Decades of outrageous terrorism that have killed thousands of innocent civilians in Israel can be black-washed to fit a heinous ANC-BDS narrative.

Palestinian terrorist, Leila Khaled, hijacked a TWA plane in 1969 on route from Rome to Athens. A year later, she attempted to hijack another plane. In this mid-flight hijacking attempt she was knocked unconscious by the El Al security personnel who killed her terrorist comrade as she tried to rush the cockpit while holding hand grenades. The plane was diverted to Heathow Airport, but she was released less than a month later by the British authorities.

In February 2105, Khaled was invited to South Africa by the BDS Movement to help in their fund-raising activities.

You know BDS is a bankrupt organization when they have to recruit terrorists to help them raise money.

In South Africa, they didn't call her a terrorist. They called her a freedom fighter.

Worse still, the South African government received this convicted Palestinian terrorist as an honored guest at their parliament, the same parliament that calls Israel an apartheid state.

Khaled is a senior leader of the PFLP. This is the terror group responsible for the cruel murders of many Israeli civilians, including the Fogel family.

In the middle of the night of March 11, 2011, PFLP terrorists entered the Fogel home, knifed the parents, Ruth and Udi, to death before stabbing the small children, Yoav aged 11, Elad aged 4, and beheading the 3 month old baby girl, Hadas, in their beds.

Khaled's PFLP was also responsible for the massacre of four rabbis and a Druze policeman at a synagogue in Jerusalem in November 2014. They butchered Jews at prayer with hatchets, meat cleavers and a rifle.

Khaled's group called them *'heroes'.*   Mahmoud Abbas paid his condolences to the families of the murderers.

PFLP are not freedom fighters. They are terrorists.

Hezbollah are not freedom fighters. They are terrorists.

Hamas are not freedom fighters. They are terrorists.

For a country like South Africa to call a hijacking and murdering Palestinian anything else but a terrorist is dangerously cynical.

It gives legitimacy to murderers.

This legitimacy was on display in October 2015 when a Hamas delegation was official guests of the African National Congress.

ANC is the leading party in South Africa. It is the party of President Jacob Zuma. Zuma received Hamas chief, Khaled Maashal, as his official guest.

During the visit Hamas and ANC signed a Memorandum of Agreement. This occurred during an upsurge of Palestinian terrorism against Israeli civilians.

Annually, in February and March, on campuses in South Africa and in the West, they organize that annual ritual of farce and fraud known as *'Israel Apartheid Week.'*

They employ an emotive misuse of words designed to demonize and delegitimize Israel – *"Israel the apartheid state," "Israel the Nazi state," "Israel the ethnic cleansing state," "Israel the racist state," "Israel the illegal occupier."*

'Israel Apartheid Week' and BDS support a Jew-free Palestine.

Isn't that racist, isn't that ethnic cleansing, isn't that Nazi?

They're acting to force this Jew-free Palestine in place of Israel, and they are supported in this effort by European parliaments, trades unions and certain church groups. Isn't that anti-Semitic?

It's certainly hypocritical.

In South Africa, *'Israel Apartheid Week'* is endorsed by Archbishop Desmond Tutu and the South African Council of Churches.

I repeat again what I told them two years ago. With what is happening across Africa and the Middle East to Christians today, my words have even more relevance.

This is addressed to you, Archbishop Tutu, and to all church leaders and campaigners that strike at Israel...

Show me a country north of Cape Town, including the whole of Africa and the whole of the Middle East, from Algeria to Afghanistan, Iraq to Iran, Syria to Sudan, one country that can be called the Rainbow Nation. That country can only be Israel.

Israel is the only country in the Middle East and much of Africa in which the Christian population is growing.

And, for the slaughter and persecution of Christians at the hands of those you support against the Jewish state, you are silent. May that be your lasting legacy!

And as for the human rights groups that target Israel, Israel is the only country in the Middle East where gays are not stigmatized or killed. Gays for Gaza? Give me a break! If you're a gay in Gaza you either stay in your closet, fearful for your life, or you escape to Tel Aviv.

As the Chief Rabbi of South Africa said, the world has lost its moral clarity, and it has lost the principled distinction between good and evil which are the bedrock of human civilization.

Nowhere is that highlighted more than in the distorted image being hurled against Israel in South Africa.

REKJAVIK – THE COLD CAPITAL OF HYPOCRISY.

Iceland is an island country located near the Arctic Circle. It tends to reach global attention when its volcanoes burst into destructive life. It reached the attention of many when, in September 2015, out of a cold blue sky, a volcano of hate erupted when Rekyavik declared a blanket boycott of everything Israeli.

Bjork Vilhelmsdottir, the Social Democrat perpetrator of Rekjavik anti-Israel boycott resolution, said that her anti-Israel boycott was formulated out of *"a desire for peace and love,"* according to the comment she made in The Rekjavik Grapevine.

She went on to say, *"I blame the Israeli government. In my opinion, they are the worst enemies of the Jewish people."* Some love, some peace!

Let me put it bluntly. Rekjavik's decision to boycott Israel was not one of love and peace. It was one of hate and divisiveness.

She then went on to tell us that she, living on an island with almost zero Jews, understands us better than we understand ourselves.

"Many people do not understand the difference between Judaism and Zionism," she lectured. *"Judaism is a faith. The other, Zionism, is a political ideology that's produced the Israeli apartheid policy."*

There you have it, straight out of the BDS playbook - Israel, the apartheid state. Judaism has nothing to do with Zionism, or Israel.

She has no idea that the aspirations of the Jewish people stands on three pillars, two of them are the Land of Israel and the People of Israel. The third leg is justice. Mrs. Vilhelmsdottir should throw away her BDS rulebook and read the Bible again before she lectures us on what constitutes Judaism.

Having her lecture us on the essence of Judaism and Zionism is like having a Nazi define for us what a Jew is. Like them, she is dead wrong in her condescending attitude.

Mrs. Vilhelmsdottir said about the blowback against the boycott, *"I didn't imagine the Israelis and Zionists in the USA would accuse us in the City Council of anti-Semitism and hate."*

First of all, Vilhelmsdottir, it wasn't Israelis or Zionists in America, it was ordinary Americans and other Jews that gave her blowback. And the fact that she protests that her act, based on her double standards, and her exclusive demonizing and delegitimizing Israel, shows how blindly Jew-hating she can be. She'll insult and compartmentalize the individual Jew while attacking the Jewish state but that, for her, is not anti-Semitism.

At the end of the day, the thing that got Rekjavik to drop the boycott was not the opposition from within the chamber, or protests from people like me. What did the trick was the threat of a counter boycott.

The Rekjavik boycott was being countered by an anti-Icelandic boycott. As Independent Party member, Halldor Halldorsson, who voted against the boycott, pointed out, Icelandic water was being removed from shelves in some American stores. Iceland was also starting to get tourism cancellations. *"The city's proposals were not consistent with our national foreign policy,"* he said.

Worse still for Iceland was the threat of economic, commercial, and tourism counter-boycotts. The city's mayor got it in the neck from the island's Prime Minister and Finance Minister. It put in jeopardy the planned construction of a Marriott's hotel in the capital. They were reminded that many of the top people at Marriott are Jewish. Others were cancelling their tourism trips to Rekjavik.

The boycott resolution was the parting act of this BDS council woman. The anti-Israel majority of the council applauded her departure by passing her resolution. When I quoted her going to serve Hamas in Gaza, I was told by the editor of the Rekjavik English newspaper that she was going there on a *"humanitarian mission."*

Speaking as an Israeli who had just experienced living under a fifty day bombardment of Hamas rockets from Gaza, plus seeing the horror of Palestinian killers emerge from their terror attack tunnels to murder my people, to say that she was going on a humanitarian mission to these people is as hypocritical as someone saying, in 1945, they were going on a humanitarian mission to Berlin and Dresden after the British bombings of these towns during war imposed on Britain by the Nazis. Somehow, the important aspect of Hamas bombings disappeared from the Rekjavik narrative.

This Icelandic lady gives us a lecture on Judaism, and the Rekjavik Council avoided any reference of the Gaza-based pledge to kill Jews while avoiding the launch of thousands of rockets and suicide bombers employed from there to achieve that aim.

This would spoil the emotional imagery which conquered up a Gaza desperate for Icelandic help that makes her *"mission"* an imperative, almost holy in its altruism.

It also makes Israel appear to be evil, more evil than any other place, more evil than China, a place where the Rekjavik mayor had paid an official visit. Rekjavik had no qualms with China's occupation of Tibet, or their appalling human rights record. They had briefly voiced criticism of its treatment of dissenters, but no thought of imposing a boycott against China. That would have spoiled an official visit.

Suddenly, with the boycott resolution, Rekjavik felt they had become more morally pure than the driven snow that covers their land, more morally pure than Tel Aviv, or even Sderot, Ashkelon, or Ashdod, whose people were confined to bomb shelters to avoid being killed by the people this lady went to sympathize with and support.

Rekjavik is now damaged. It has to recover from being the cold capital of hypocrisy.

BDS LIES, INTIMIDATION, VIOLENCE. BRITISH ACADEMIA 2016.

The dogma of unreasoned hate pervades the atmosphere in seats of higher learning and research as campaigners for an end to Israel make dangerous inroads into the once hallowed hallways of British academia.

The beginning of 2016 saw the nadir of freedom of speech at King College London, a once proud bastion of open debate and intellectual honesty.

When Ami Ayalon, former director of Israel's Shin Bet and currently a left-wing pro-peace activist, began his talk in a small room on the UK campus on January 20, protesters set off fire alarms, broke a window, threw chairs and physically assaulted a female attending the talk as they screamed abuse.

They interrupted an event organized by the Kings College Israel Society designed to find a peaceful solution to the Israel-Palestinian problem with chants of *"From the river to the sea Palestine will be free"* clearly indicating that their cause is not peace but an end to Israel.

Amazingly, although a heavy police force was required to put down the violence no arrests were made.

This type of intimidation and violence is becoming increasingly common on campuses as intolerant radicals close down thought and debate that conflict with their agenda. There is little colloquy left in academia for Israeli advocates.

This sorry state of affairs is moving into the realm of research. At the same time as the Zionist group at Kings College was being attacked, seventy one British doctors called to expel the Israeli Medical Association from the world body. The reason given was that Israeli doctors were carrying out *"medical torture"* on Palestinian patients.

One wonders where men of supposed intellect not only get this nonsense but use it to ban some of the world's finest medical minds.

Staggering, the urge to ban Israeli medical researchers and scientists from the World Medical Association, based on fraudulent accusations, occurred at the same time that Israeli medical scientists announced a breakthrough in the treatment of ALS.

Until now, there had been no significant success in slowing the progression of Lou Gehrig's disease. But now, thanks to the research conducted at Israel's Hadassah Medical Center, it seems that collecting stem cells from the patient's bone marrow and injecting it into the patient's spinal fluid not only stops the degeneration but actually reverses the process. Notable improvement has been recorded in the neurological functions of the test patients.

It is unacceptable that a blind political bias against the Jewish state has led to the situation where expert Israeli voices can no longer be heard in Britain and that these haters are dominating the academic conversation.

What can we learn from these British-based provocations?

You can't have peace without truth. As we see with the Palestinian refusal to even negotiate and the UK attempt to boycott Israeli academics and to close down free speech, you can't have truth or peace without conversation.

We also learn that both the Palestinians and their global supporters reject the notion of the existence of a Jewish state to the point of violence.

Israel will continue to prosper and thrive. The benefits emanating out of Israeli academia and research centers will continue to benefit a world that is noisily hurling abuse and lies against us.

The problem lies with the closing of the academic mind in Britain linked to its rejection of Jewish thought and expression. When academic minds refuse to listen, the campus becomes a place of dogma. When it becomes a place of dogma it is no longer academia, a place of meeting of minds and open conversation. It is a harm inflicted upon itself, more than upon us.

The development of the Israeli academic genius and our desire for peace will continue to shine through the black clouds of hate and negativity we are witnessing within the UK and, sadly, on campuses elsewhere.

THE FAITHFUL ROOTS OF CHRISTIAN ZIONISTS.

Like it or not, Israel is the shining light of humanity in a desert of darkness and oppression. Christians, who are the target in areas void of Jews, should pick up that torch and shine it in all the dark corners of affliction.

Christian Zionists, rooted to their faithful interpretation of the Bible, identify and stand firmly with the Jewish people in the land of Israel. They know that, beyond the Bible, the legitimate rights of the Jewish people to sovereignty in the land far outweigh any other claims.

This support is not something new. This was the common understanding of leading Christians at the turn of the 20th Century who saw the return of the Jewish people to their land at that time as an inevitable and natural turn of events. It was a phenomenon that displaced no one. In fact, it attracted a mass Arab migration much akin to what we see in Europe today.

In the London of 1840, Lord Palmerston, the British Foreign Secretary, strongly recommended to the Ottoman government that ruled over Palestine that they should *"hold out every just encouragement to the Jews of Europe to return to Palestine."*

It was indisputable that allowing European Jews looking to rejoin their indigenous co-religionists in the Holy Land made perfect sense in the sphere of universal ideas and enlightenment.

In 1853, Lord Shaftesbury coined the phrase describing a barren Palestine and the yearning of the Jewish people for a return to Zion as *"a land without a people for people without a land."*

Back in 1891, the Reverend William E. Blackstone, presented US President Benjamin Harrison with a petition for the reinstatement of Jews to

Palestine. Among the signatories were John D. Rockefeller, J.P.Morgan, and Cardinal Gibbons.

In 1894, Scottish preacher and scholar, Sir George Adam Smith, published *The Historical Geography of the Holy Land.* This book was to influence and helped General Sir Edmund Allenby in his 1917 battles in the Holy Land to defeat the Ottoman Empire. In his authoritative work, Smith insisted that the Ottomans had to be pushed out of Palestine to be replaced by the Jews. His thought was premised on one overriding consideration, that it was the Jews *"who had given to Palestine everything it has ever had of value to the world."*

Some would argue that this is precisely what Israel is giving to the world today.

Conservative Christians have a firm belief in the imperative of the Jewish return to Zion. In 1909, Cyrus Ingerson Schofield, a Protestant, edited the King James Version of the Bible by adding extensive footnotes that emphasized the then present and future role of Israel in world history.

The Balfour Declaration of November 1917 whereby the British Government announced that it favored *"the establishment in Palestine of a national home for the Jewish people'* was the most important act premised by Christian Zionism.

David Lloyd George, British Prime Minister between the years 1916 to 1922, supported the establishment of a Jewish state in Palestine not out of some cynical political maneuvering but out of a deeply held conviction that it was the right thing to do. The son of a Welsh Baptist schoolmaster, he once said, *"I was taught in school more about the history of the Jews than about my own land."*

One of his aides describing this phenomenon said, *"Bible reading and Bible thinking England was the only country where the desire of the Jews to return to their ancient homeland was a natural aspiration not to be denied."*

Jews and Christians today share a common enemy. That enemy is radical Islam. Islam has a rabid hatred of anything Jewish but it also has an open contempt for Christianity. Neither Christians nor Jews, including Israel, hold any motivation to conquer Muslim lands not to deprive Muslims of their right to pray. Jews have no proselyting intent. Judaism is the most difficult religion to break into. Converting non-believers is far from being a Jewish obsession. Islam has nothing to fear from conversion-motivated rabbis. There is no such thing. Let a Muslim try to covert to Judaism. Impossible would be an understated word. The reason radical Islam hates Jews and Christians is not because we are out to get them and convert them. The opposite is true. It is because we have no interest in joining their club. That's what makes them livid. They cannot tolerate a world where not everyone is Muslim. It drives them crazy.

This is the reason why Christians and Jews should be allies and that Israel should remain the bastion of their support.

THE NAKBA BULLSHIT. IT'S A SELF INFLICTED CATASTROPHE.

The Zionist enterprise in the Holy Land of the 19th Century was dynamically developed by the industrious Jews. This attracted an Arab immigration like a magnet which increased the Arab population west of the Jordan River.

The other larger parts of what had been Palestine, including what was to become Transjordan, as well as Syria, Iraq and Egypt, were still backwaters, offering little employment or development to its people. The Jews employed this immigrant source of labor despite the fact that acts of violence and murder were committed by Arabs on Jews. Jews in the land suffered decades of bloodshed and murder at the hands of the Arabs going back to the massacres in Safed and Hebron in 1929. So it continued, including murderous raids by what were called *"fedayeen"*, an early form of Arab terrorism.

When the Jewish State of Israel was brought into being at the United Nations in 1947 it was roundly rejected by the Arabs.

In 1948, the fledgling Jewish state was attacked by heavily armed and trained Arab armies. The war was initiated by the Arabs for the purpose of driving Jews they did not kill into the sea. Victory over the newly-born state seemed inevitable. Combined forces from Iraq, Syria, Jordan, Egypt, supported by arms and soldiers from Lebanon, Yemen, and Saudi Arabia, attacked the undermanned and barely armed Jewish nation.

Less than three years after the horrors of the Holocaust Jews faced another genocide, this time at the hands of the Arabs. The outcome, however, was a resounding defeat for the Arabs that left Israel in situ over a larger territory and the local displaced Arabs in despair.

The Arab hatred of the Jews and their desire to remove the Jewish presence from the Middle East was not erased. The new narrative purported to give the lie that the Jews woke up one day and decided to execute ethnic cleansing against the indigenous Arab population. Not true. The intended ethnic cleansing of 1948 would have been of the Jews at the hands of the invading Arab armies.

Another myth is that the Palestinian refugee problem is the fault of the Jews. Also untrue.

Anti-Israel activism includes a narrative of the *'Arab Nakba.'* This notion of history is led by the Palestinian Authority and taken up by all and sundry on their side of the political divide.

Basically, it tells a tale of Jews driving out Arabs, forcing them into refugee status since 1948 and in which they remain today. The Palestinians are the only class that demands retaining refugee status into their fifth, and soon sixth, generation.

This traditional lie has been allowed to grow in the Arab and anti-Israel world.

Once a year, Arabs commemorate a time when many uprooted themselves from what had become Israel. It was a time when Arab armies invaded the nascent state of Israel. It was this incident that created a refugee problem that is unsolved to this day. They call this event The Nakba. *("the Catastrophe.")*

At its core they are not commemorating their upheaval. They are not marking their dispossession. Rather, they are campaigning for the elimination of Israel. They are protesting over the creation of the Jewish State of Israel, an event that occurred before the personal tragedies of many Arabs. They do not use this day to mourn the tragic events of the 1948 war. Rather it is an emotional and public outpouring of their rejection of Israel, a rejection that began decades ago, and will continue beyond the Palestinian claim for statehood in the United Nations General

Assembly. They rejected Israel in the United Nations in 1947. They will continue to do so after the United Nations. The Nakba parades and slogans accuse Israel of their *"calamity"*. It is a self-inflicted tragedy caused by the Arabs themselves.

With the flight of so many local Arabs from the area of conflict came the flight from fact into fantasy with the development of a political myth, a rewriting of history, to be used to delegitimize Israel and accuse it of crimes it did not commit. It is a dangerous effort by the Palestinian leadership to create a history out of a lie for a malevolent agenda.

The myth that the Palestinian refugee problem is the fault of the Jews is untrue.

They left their homes at the orders of the Arab High Command, not by Jews who, generally, implored them to stay. This is easily proven by anyone who cares to do the research.

Emile Ghoury was the Secretary of the Palestinian Arab Higher Committee. Here is what he told the London Telegraph in August 1948. It was later repeated in the Beirut Telegraph on September 6, 1948;

"The fact that there are these refugees is a direct consequence of the acts of the Arab states in opposing partition and the Jewish state."

The London Economist confirmed this view on October 2 of the same year;

"The most potent factor was the announcements made over the air by the Arab-Palestinian Higher Executive urging all Haifa Arabs to quit. It was clearly intimated that Arabs who remained and accepted Jewish protection would be regarded as renegades."

The paper was merely confirming what the Haifa District HQ of the British Police reported on April 26, 1948;

"Every effort is being made by the Jews to persuade the Arab populace to stay and carry on with their normal lives."

It was not confined to Haifa. It was a widespread command by the Arabs that created their own Nakba. As the Near East Arabic broadcasting station in Cyprus wired on April 3, 1949;

"It must not be forgotten that the Arab Higher Committee encouraged the refugee's flight from their homes in Jaffa, Haifa and Jerusalem."

As one such refugee reported to the Jordanian paper, Al Difaa, on September 6, many years later in 1954;

"The Arab governments told us 'get out so we can get in.' So, we got out but they didn't get in."

And if you want a relevant voice on the topic of the Palestinian Nakba, how about Mahmoud Abbas himself who wrote in the official journal of the PLO in Beirut, Falastin al-Thawra, in March 1976;

"The Arab armies entered Palestine to protect the Palestinians from the Zionist tyranny, but instead they abandoned them, forced them to emigrate and to leave their homeland, imposed upon them a political and ideological blockade and threw them into prisons similar to the ghettos in which the Jews used to live in Eastern Europe."

Many years later, Abbas reconfirmed his charges that *"the Arab states are the cause of the Palestinian refugee problem."* Wall Street Journal, June 5, 2003.

The Nakba, then, must point directly at the Arab leadership and not at Israel. It is a tragedy that thousands of Arabs remain in Arab refugee camps to this day. It is a tragedy perpetuated by Arab nations in conjunction with the United Nations who chose to keep them in this status for a political purpose in order to use them as pawns in their ongoing campaign against Israel.

The obscenity of the decades old Arab refugee problem is completely down to the failure of the surrounding Arab nations with the collusion of the United Nations who are both guilty of perpetuating this human tragedy.

Juxtapositioned with this Arab catastrophe were the tragedies of the Jewish populations of the neighboring Arab states. At the time that the Arab armies were attacking the newly formed Israel, Jews were being attacked, killed, and displaced in most of the Arab countries. Some statistics show that two hundred thousand more Jews were driven out of their homes in the Muslim countries than Arabs that left Israel. The big difference was that these Jews found shelter in Israel where they were welcomed, absorbed, nurtured, and made useful citizens.

No Nakba exists for Jewish refugees. Neither does the State of Israel go begging to the United Nations to keep them in victimhood and permanent sponsorship. Self-pride and an independence spirit is a Jewish value that prevents this sense of self-loathing and hatred of the other. What could have been a Jewish Nakba was turned into a Jewish humanitarian success story and a glorious example to the world.

This is another shining example of the humanity of the Jewish state compared to the dark history of Arab inhumanity against their own people.

Nakba is an Arabic word meaning *"disaster."* But the Muslims should celebrate rather than mourn this event since this event was foreseen in their Koran.

Arabs left the Arabian Peninsula after the death of Mohammed in 632. They invaded and settled in various countries where they forced people to accept Islam, thereby creating Muslim states with one exception – the land of the Jews.

The Koran repeatedly warns the Muslims, in Surah 5:21, 7:137, 10:93, 17:104 and 28:4, based on translations by Abdullah Yusufali, that Allah allocated this land to the Jews.

No Muslim state was ever established in Palestine and the first Arab attempt to invade the land by multiple Muslim armies ended in defeat not only in 1948 but repeatedly since.

So the Arabs should not attempt to go against the will of Allah by attacking Israel, the Jewish state, for it directly goes against their god's will. They should leave Israel alone and heed the 1948 and 1967 events as a foretelling of the Koran in which they believe so passionately and religiously.

THE PALESTINIAN CAUSE IS THE BIGGEST POLITICAL FRAUD IN HISTORY.

When the Arabs lost five aggressive wars against Israel after they had rejected the United Nations Partition Plan they reframed the conflict into the Israel-Palestinian conflict. They came up with a new narrative. The land is Palestine and the Jews are colonialists. They invented their identity and history and erased any Jewish connection to the land. They said they would kill until they liberate every inch of that land. They have not given up on their desire to eliminate the Jewish state.

Now Israel is always projected as being anti-peace. So why is it that consecutive prime ministers including Rabin, Peres, Barak, Olmert, Sharon, Netanyahu have all said we are prepared to accept and recognize the rights of the Palestinians to a state of their own? Has any Palestinian leader said they recognize the rights of the Jewish people, or our historic connections to this land? Where did the word Judaism come from? From Judea. Where is Judea? Judea is in what was, and is again, the Jewish state.

What has happened is not peace. The Arabs have taken this concession to mean *"Ah! You see. The Jews admit that the land is not theirs. They must leave our land now!"*

You see the twist that has been put on the peace gesture. So when you say, *"let Israel pull back even further"* you have become an advocate for the Palestinian cause. You are admitting that the land is theirs and we have no right, no legitimacy, for being there. They have said that we have no legitimacy in any of the land. In fact, they totally reject the notion that we have legitimacy anywhere. Mahmoud Abbas said, *"We will never accept the legitimacy of a Jewish state, not in a thousand years!"* How do you have peace if you don't recognize the legitimacy of the other? Peace is presented as a one way street. Palestinians make demands and Israel makes concessions. Peace is a two way street. Both sides must make concessions. Both sides must show that they are conditioning their people for peace, not confrontation.

Fighting against the delegitimizers is fighting for the conditions that facilitate peacemaking. Fighting against Palestinian incitement and hatred is fighting for the conditions for peace.

Match *'Israel Apartheid Week'* with *'Israel Peace Week'*. Draw the real peace makers away from the extremists and into your camp. They have to decide whose side they are really on. This isolates the radicals. Their strategy will backfire on them. Then teach your new supporters what Zionism really is about, what Israel really is about, with ongoing workshops, camps, lectures, study courses, and visits to Israel. Show them that Israel is far from being a racist society, and show them the regimes that really are racist.

Teach them what American civil rights leader, Vernon Jordan, said in 1975 after the Durban *'Zionism is Racism'* resolution. He said that *"smearing the racist label on Zionism is an insult to intelligence. Black people who recognize the code words since we've been victimized by code words can easily smell out the fact that Zionism in this context is a code word for anti-Semitism."*

You need to show them Arab discrimination. Show them Arab discrimination against Christians, Kurds, Sudanese, Yazidis, and Jews, even against Palestinians in their midst. There you'll find the real apartheid against Palestinians. The Arabs are the leading proponents of discrimination and racism. Show me a Jew in Saudi Arabia! I rest my case.

Eldridge Cleaver, the Black Panther activist, said, *"I was shocked because of all the people in the world, the Jews have not only suffered particularly from racist persecution, they have done more than any other people in history to expose and condemn racism. To condemn the Jewish survival doctrine of Zionism as racism is a travesty upon the truth."*

Martin Luther King, the American civil rights hero, the Mandela of America, knew what Israel's battle was all about. He said, and I quote, *"Israel's right to exist as a state in security is uncontestable."*

On March 25, 1968, less than two weeks before his tragic death, King said, *"peace for Israel means security, and we must stand with all our might to protect its right to exist, its territorial integrity. I see Israel as one of the great outposts of democracy in the world, and a marvelous example of what can be done, how desert can be transformed into an oasis of brotherhood and democracy. Peace for Israel means security and that security must be a reality."*

He went on *"I solemnly pledge to do my utmost to uphold the fair name of the Jews because bigotry in any form is an affront to us all."*

There are millions of black Christians who share King's desire to uphold the fair name of the Jews and they are ready to pledge that Israel's right to exist is uncontestable. Like him, they are pragmatic realists.

And to take this issue further, King said, when posed with a hostile question about Zionism, that *"When people criticize Zionists they mean Jews, you are talking anti-Semitism."*

Clarence B. Jones, a friend and advisor to King, opposed the anti-Israel comments from Al Sharpton and Jesse Jackson by pointing to what Martin Luther King had said after the Six Day War in 1967 when King warned that anti-Semitism would soon be disguised as anti-Zionism.

He was unambiguously opposed to Israel-bashing. He recognized Israel's right to exist as being the centrality of the conflict. He would have been appalled at the avowed anti-Zionism of people like Omar Barghouti leader of the BDS campaign. He clearly saw the ultimate aim of BDS, one that was disowned by none other than Norman Finkelstein, no great lover of Israel and a once BDS advocate.

Finkelstein admitted that the BDS Movement is a dishonest bunch of left wing radicals whose aim is the end of Israel. In his words *"it's not an accidental and unwitting omission that BDS does not mention Israel. You know that and I know that. It's not like they're 'Oh, we forgot to mention it.' They won't mention it because they know it will split the movement, because there's a large segment of the movement that wants to eliminate Israel."*

Are you going to reach a broad public that hear the Israeli side say, 'BDS want to destroy us?' No, you're not. And frankly you know you shouldn't. You shouldn't reach a broad public because you're dishonest. And I wouldn't trust those people if I had to live in this state. I wouldn't. It's dishonesty."

In response to Finkelstein's remarks the editor of the *Al-Akhbar* English paper and website said, *"Finkelstein rightly asks whether the real aim of BDS is to bring down the State of Israel. Here, I agree with him that it is. That should be stated as an unambiguous goal. There should not be any equivocation on the subject. Justice and freedom for the Palestinians are incompatible with the existence of the state of Israel."*

So there you have it. The Palestinian cause is the biggest political fraud in history. It's not a state alongside Israel. It is a state in place of Israel.

Faced with this reality do you really expect Israel to grant them more land, more territory, and put our head on the chopping block of international appeasement? To do so would be like feeding Israeli lambs to Palestinian lions in the hope that the lions will wake up in the morning as vegetarians. It simply won't happen. They have the taste for Jewish blood and they want it all.

What are the chances of this Palestine casting off its corrupt and extremist leaders and become a pragmatic and truly democratic regime?

Sadly, that's not at all likely. And, based on this reality, Israel must not be compelled to take further hazardous steps that will endanger its people.

THE PERVERTED LANGUAGE OF THE PALESTINIAN NARRATIVE.

Palestinians persecute Christians for being Christians. That's religious persecution. That's apartheid. It's happening in Palestinian-controlled towns, and yet some Christian leaders call Israel an apartheid racist state. That's anti-Semitism. It's also downright stupid.

When Christian leaders slander and abuse the Jewish state in support of those who are abusing and assaulting Christians, even as those Christians find refuge in the Jewish state and elsewhere, that's disgusting hypocrisy and anti-Semitism.

In 2013, the Church of Scotland announced that Israel does not belong to the Jewish people. That's Christian anti-Semitism.

In early 2016, the United Methodist Church announced it was to boycott Israeli banks. What was this foolish decision all about? It is the Palestinians who are persecuting Christians, not Israel. Just ask the thousands of Christians who have fled once Christian Bethlehem. Or ask Father Gabriel Naddaf, the Christian pastor from the Galilee, who is leading his flock in a movement to reclaim the Aramaic heritage for Israeli Christians in defiance of the intimidation and threats he has been receiving from his Muslim Arab neighbors in and around Nazareth. Ask him where in Israel the racism is coming from.

The lie of Palestinian territory since 1967 has become a diplomatic and academic *'truth'* that drives a political agenda. Any solution built on lies is doomed to failure but with dangerous consequences.

Palestinians invoke UN Resolution 242 for their cause, but *'Palestine'* isn't mentioned or referred to at all. Read it!   Conclusion – they have no claim at all based on 242. Saying that they do is a lie.

Arab or Islamic Palestine isn't mentioned once in the bible or any other history books.   Jerusalem and Palestine aren't mentioned at all in the Koran.

The abuse of language turns racist terrorist Palestinians into victims, and Israel the victim into a guilty party.

Palestinians regularly portray Jews as descendants of apes and pigs in their official media and official PA religious broadcasts. This in itself is anti-Semitic. They insist that their state will be entirely Judenrein, a land cleared of Jews. This is racist and anti-Semitic. Yet, they accuse Israel of racism.

The Palestinian Authority tried to accuse Israel of desecrating holy sites on the Temple Mount when it was their Palestinian hooligans that stormed the Al Aqsa mosque on the Temple Mount, tore up the furniture to use as barricades and clubs, stored and hurled rocks, firebombs and chairs at the security forces sent to restore law and order at this holy place.

WHEN WILL ISRAELI VICTIMS OF PALESTINIAN TERROR GET THEIR DAY IN COURT?

On April 1, 2015, the Jerusalem Post had a glaring front page story about a borderless, undemocratic, questionably lawless entity known as *'Palestine'* applying to becoming a member of the International Criminal Court.

The PLO was quoted as saying that *"It is war crimes and war criminals that undermine peace efforts."*

They are the ones who commit war crimes. They are the ones who are war criminals.

The PLO also said that the decision to join the ICC *"reflects Palestine's unwavering commitment to peace, universal values, and determination to provide protection for its people and hold those responsible for the crimes they have committed."*

Could a Palestinian Authority guilty of decades of incitement, violence, terrorism, that left thousands of Israelis dead or injured, have decided to join the world criminal court to bring charges against itself?

Maybe, in a fit of moral clarity, they had decided the only way to peace was a complete reform of their violent terroristic tendencies and had decided to throw themselves on the mercy of the ICC to investigate their war and human rights crimes, both against innocent Israelis and their own people?

Despite the repeated rockets and mortar attacks, over ten thousand in number, against Israeli civilian targets, despite launching terror attacks against Israeli civilians many gruesomely executed, they seem to be oblivious to the nature of the heinous crimes they commit.

Shurat HaDin, the Israel law NGO, has filed war crimes charges against Hamas on behalf of 26 Americans for their deliberate firing of rockets at Ben Gurion Airport during the 2014 Hamas-initiated Gaza conflict.

One piece of evidence that, hopefully, will convict Hamas on these charges was the statement of their spokesman, Sami Abu Zuhri, who had triumphantly admitted that *"the success of Hamas in closing Israeli air space is a great victory for the resistance, and is a crown of Israel's failure."*

The Palestinian Authority and the PLO became members of the ICC in The Hague on April 1, 2015. But the Palestinian Authority and the PLO were found guilty of terrorism charges in a New York court on February 23, 2015 in a class action suit brought by the families of ten Americans killed by them in a series of deadly attacks that killed 33 people and wounded more than 400 others in Israel.

Let's be brutally honest. It has been Palestinian Arabs that have introduced to the world of terrorism plane hijackings, car bombings, suicide bombings and terrorist rocket and missile use, all against innocent civilians while hiding behind their own civilians.

So much for Palestinian statements of an *"unwavering commitment to peace and universal values."*

As with all their commitments, it's all smoke and mirrors. It's Palestinian war crimes and war criminals that undermine peace efforts, and it is time that the international community opened its eyes to this truth.

When are Israeli victims of Palestinian terror going to have their day in court? Why is it that only the American victims of Palestinian crimes who are receiving justice?

Although many Palestinian terrorists have been arrested, tried in a military court and imprisoned, not one Israeli family has received closure by having criminal charges brought against the Palestinian Authority, the PLO, Hamas, or any of their leaders, despite the mountain of evidence against them. Not one of them has received a shekel in compensation for the loss and damage brought down on them by these guilty parties to terrorism who are now claiming victimhood in The Hague.

We live in a morally twisted world but true justice, real justice, will only be served when the thousands of Israeli victims of Palestinian terror have their day in court.

BDS LIES WHEN THEY SAY THEY STAND FOR JUSTICE.

You can't say you are making a moral argument when you talk about peace in the Middle East but conveniently forget the multiple times since 1937 the Palestinian Arab leadership has rejected peace offers. You are absolving them of their responsibility.

You can't talk about violence between Israelis and Palestinians without including Palestinian incitement and glorification of the discriminate killing of Israeli civilians and the rewarding of these cold-blooded killers with hefty salaries.

You can't ignore thousands of rockets launched by Palestinians against Israeli civilians. Nor can you ignore the fact that Palestinian children died in Gaza while digging terror tunnels for Hamas who use them to send their terrorists into Israel to kill Israeli children.

You cannot ignore actions and consequences.

BDS talks about human rights, but ignores the Palestinian use of civilian human shields in Gaza. A child in Gaza is 100% at the mercy of Hamas and their ideology.

Hamas can store and fire missiles in a child's house or school without BDS reproach. Hamas can use this child's body to defend its terrorists.

You can't conduct an honest conversation about Palestinian human rights and forget the Palestinians oppressed by Hamas and by the profoundly corrupt Palestinian Authority.

You talk about racism and ignore the Hamas culture of genocide against Jews.

How can you talk about racism and take no notice about Mahmoud Abbas's anti-Semitic statements.

There can be no honest discussion about justice if the BDS continues to evade the total rejection of Jewish rights to self-determination.

You can't call for self-determination of one side while stripping the right to self-determination of the other side, and call it justice.

It is all so contrary to the values that BDS say they are promoting. This is so left of justice that it is no justice at all.

SOME CLOSING THOUGHTS.

WORDS MATTER!

It begins with words. Hateful words, words that are meant to demonize and delegitimize. People ignored the words of Hitler's speeches and his *'Mein Kampf,'* words that led to the death of Anne Frank, and six million others.

People are ignoring the words of Palestinian Hamas in their media and in their infamous charter. Words like, *'Oh Muslim! There's a Jew hiding behind me. Come out and kill him!'*

People ignored the words of Arafat and Abbas, words that incite, words that erase any Jewish belonging or heritage, words that position a world without Jews, without Israel.

No. I'm not an islamophobe. Neither is this Jewish paranoia. After thousands of years of Jewish persecution, we dare not wait until they spill Jewish blood before we are allowed to point at the perpetrators and call them anti-Semites.

Our instincts are sharper now. We know now, as Jews, that if someone says they intend to kill us we believe him – and that applies to the messianic terrorist Mullahs of Iran.

WHERE THEY BOYCOTT BOOKS, THEY EVENTUALLY BURN THEM.

AND WHERE THEY BURN BOOKS, THEY EVENTUALLY BURN PEOPLE.

I visited Berlin. I went to Bebelplatz. This was the place where, at the orders and in the presence of Josef Goebbels, the Germans ransacked the national library and burnt 20,000 books, books written by Jews, books about Jews, burnt in Bebelplatz square. It was the start of Kristallnacht.

In that square today there is a bronze plaque on the ground. Engraved upon it is a quotation by German philosopher, Heinrich Heine, written in 1823, one hundred and ten years before Kristallnacht, one hundred and ninety plus years before today. It says,

"Where they burn books, they eventually burn people."

My wife's family was herded into a Lithuanian synagogue on Rosh Hashanah, the Jewish New Year, by the Nazis.

The door was locked and the synagogue set on fire. My wife's family never saw Yom Kippur –the Day of Atonement.

It is happening again. This time in the Middle East. And the only reason they are not burning Jews is because the Jews befell an earlier misfortune of being beaten, killed and driven out of these Muslim lands. They found refuge in Israel, the Jewish state.

So they are burning and beheading Christians instead.

First they come for the Saturday people. Then they come for the Sunday people.

If the world fails to find its moral compass, as it failed to do so in Munich with Chamberlain and Hitler, we Jews will once again face an evil determined to kill us, to burn us, to destroy us.

They are already threating and trying to do that, and they are aided and abetted by BDS intellectual hooligans and bullies.

We Jews face a world that's eager to demonize and delegitimize us just as they did in Nazi Europe, just as they did in the Spanish Inquisition, just as they did at the dawn of Islam.

IT'S THE WAY THEY PRACTICE THOUGHT TODAY.

In the end, it's not about Israel or Jews at all. It is the way they practice thought in today's twisted and dangerous world.

So stop for a second and imagine a world without Israel and the enormous contribution that this tiny Jewish state has given to an unappreciative, hostile, and cynical world.

Then go further and look at the Middle East and Africa.

Look at their deplorable living standards, their ideologies, their attitudes, their intolerance to those who dare disagree with them, not willing to live like them.

Imagine what our world would look like if our enemies succeed.

Who would rather live in Iran, Iraq, Libya, Syria, Saudi Arabia, Afghanistan, or a Palestinian Hamastan?

Who needs Israel?

Let's be honest – the world does.

BDS LIES ABOUT RACISM AND COLOR.

BDS LIES when it accuses White Israel of oppressing Black or Brown Palestinians. They often use this imagery to recruit minority sympathizers to their cause and to inject false imagery of a racist imperialist Israel. Oh, how they like to play the race card against Israel.

So let's be accurate here. *'White'* Westerners are a minority in Israel compared to immigrants from *'brown'* Middle Eastern and *'black'* African countries.
The non-racist character of Israel can be seen in the blending of black Ethiopians, the browns of Yemen, Tunisia, Iraq, Egypt, Syria and Morocco with the white of Europe, America, Canada and Australia who have made Israel their home.

The Edward Said formula of white oppression of colored Palestinian people simply won't wash when you actually check Israel's demography.

SLY ANTI-SEMITISM.

Europe has always been a place where it's been easy to push a Jew around. Now, the rhetoric of anti-Israelism has filtered down to the neighborhood bully.

The negative talk about Israel gives him the opportunity to spit on his local Jew. It gives him the license to hurl insults, and worse.

What this thug is doing, as he assaults the local Jew, is saying, *"See! I said you Jews were bastards!"*

In the past he would have shouted, *"Get the hell out of here! Go to Palestine where you belong!"* Now he has the chance to bully the local Jew by jeering, *"Get the hell out of Palestine! You don't belong there!"*

Of course, he doesn't want them in his location. Let them wander the face of the earth. Homeless, stateless, the eternal Wandering Jew.

Then there are the others. The ones that say, *"I'm not anti-Semitic. Some of my best friends are Jews. It's just Israelis I hate."*

They object to Israel. They are sympathetic to the Palestinians. But their purported love of the Palestinians is disingenuous.

If truth be told, they can't stand the Arabs at all. And the hole in their narrative is they share the decades old violent, war-like, terror-laden, anti-Semitism of the Arab world, now spearheaded by the Palestinian cause, has murdered Jews incessantly.

This awful history is a negative, void of any redeeming feature. It continues to this day, still an empty space in the tainted monologue against the Jew and the Jewish state.

Then there are those whose intellectual capacity goes little further than throwing vacuous, easily disprovable, political insults at Israel.

You know the type I mean. Israel, the fascist country, Israel, the apartheid state, Israel, practicing ethnic cleansing, Israel, practicing genocide, Israel, the baby killers, Israel, the Nazi. The list goes on and on.

Ever tried discussing the issue with shallow-minded bigots? You can't get past one insult before their response is yet another. There is no substance you can debate with them. Their mind has been stuffed with the polemic of bias and hate.

When Israelis were being slaughtered by Arafat's murderous henchmen and suicide bombers the world expressed little sympathy.

They went silent. No expression of horror over pictures of dead Jews on buses or in cafes. Just silence.

Then Israelis began to defend themselves. They went after the terrorists, and the rumbles began to be heard, the grumbles began to be heard.

Jews fighting back make certain people's attitude change. For them a Jew winning is a bit of a problem. It gives them the opportunity to express their opinion.

It's an opinion that expresses itself as, *"those Jews picking on that poor Arab!"* No context. No background. Not factual. Just a selective anti-Jewish statement that slips so easily into the conversation, into the newspapers, and onto the TV screens.

It's what I call *"sly anti-Semitism."*

They can't believe they are anti-Semites even as they utter profoundly Jew-hating comments that slip so easily from the tongue. After all, expressing sympathy for the poor Arabs can't be bad, can it?

The European Jewish Congress had to call for the suspension of a Maltese European Union official, a Stefan Grech, in July 2015 for publicly calling a woman *"a dirty Jew"* and telling her that *"Hitler should have killed all the Jews."*

Grech told the Time of Malta newspaper that *"I am not a racist. I have Jewish and black friends,"* proving the point that anti-Semites don't know they are anti-Semites even as they hurl anti-Semitic rhetoric at Jews.

A minister in the Greek government resigned in September 2015, less than 48 hours after being appointed as Deputy Transport Minister, as a result of the outcry that following a series of his anti-Semitic tweets.

One of the tweets accused New York Jews of not showing up for work at the World Trade Center thereby subscribing to the conspiracy theory that Jews (others say Israelis) were behind the 9/11 terrorist attacks in America.

Dimitris Kammenos had earlier posted a Facebook picture of the gates of Auschwitz with the words *"We stay in Europe"* in place of the Nazi *"Arbeit macht frei."*

This Greek Kammenos is not related to Panos Kammenos, the Defense Minister, who, during the election campaign falsely claimed that *"Jews don't pay taxes."*

Is it any wonder that members of certain Greek political parties occasionally erupt with anti-Jewish stereotyping but express their anti-Israel bile more openly, and more frequently?

Earlier in this book I wrote about the Malmo Syndrome that I later renamed the Matisyahu Symptom. It is the meeting point where latent anti-Semitism picks on Israel, and where Israel is exploited to express inbred Jew hatred.

In August 2015, the British police received a criminal complaint. Alison Chabloz, a musician, performed the banned neo-Nazi quenelle salute and suggested that Nazi gas chambers did not exist. As her actions and the charges gained publicity, she blogged that her gesture was a *"massive up yours"* as a reaction to being *"hounded online by a small group of hard-line Zionists."*

Earlier, she had claimed that *"Anne Frank's diary was mostly fabricated"* and that British organizations teaching about the Holocaust were *"indoctrinating children."* Oh, those nasty lying Jews!

This Jew-hating artist courts publicity by posting controversial anti-Jewish statements. As she posted, *"All publicity is good, and it's time more people started standing up to Zionist bullies."*

It's not too difficult to understand that Chabloz uses the term *"Zionists"* to mean Jews and vice versa. There is little difference between the two. She even signed off with the hashtag *#FreePalestine* to prove my point. So it goes with most of the BDS mob.

In September 2015, a German mayor, Albrecht Schroter, who supports a boycott of Israeli products (but refuses to throw away his phone or his computer) blamed Israel for the Syrian refugee problem that is plaguing Germany.

Reinhard Schramm, the chairman of the Jewish community of Thuringia state in which the town of Jena sits, claimed that Schroter *"fosters anti-Semitism."*

This was denied by Markus Giebe in a contradictory manner. The deputy head of the Jena City Council told the *Jerusalem Post* that *"Israel is not responsible for the refugee crisis"* and that he didn't believe that Schroter was a left-wing anti-Semite. However, Giebe signed a petition from the Jena Jusos group, a young adult organization of the Social Democrats that criticized Schroter for contributing *"unwittingly to make anti-Semitic thinking respectable in our society."*

And who says you can't be Jewish and an anti-Semite when attacking Israel. With our Jewish ingenuity even that is something we do better than the goyim.

The Israeli Embassy in Berlin came down hard on a German bank for sponsoring an event calling for the destruction of Israel.

The embassy blasted the bank and the organizers *"for allowing an opponent of the existence of Israel, who has likened the Jewish State to the Third Reich, to deliver a talk entitled 'Jew against Zionism.'"* They added, *"We regret that certain organizations provide a platform for hatred."*

The bank in question was the Sparkasse savings bank that, it is claimed, played a financial role under the Third Reich. The *Ostfriesen* newspaper went as far as writing about an exhibition that showed *"Sparkesse loyally served the Nazi regime."*

The invited speaker was Lillian Rosengarten from New York who spoke at the bank's Duren office. She is a member of an anti-Zionist network and accused Israel on the town's museum's website of the tired tropes of *"ethnic cleansing," "racism,"* and *"apartheid."*

To prove my point that you can be Jewish and anti-Semitic, this lady blamed her hatred on Zionism. She said that *"Zionism has been successful in activating a growth in anti-Semitism"* without stopping to think that Jew haters were the ones who were using their anti-Semitism against the notion of a Jewish state, and that she had joined their gang.

People positioned as critics of Israel turned their backs on her. The Protestant community cancelled a talk she was to have given because, in the past, she had compared Israel to the Nazism. Even a Green Party politician, Hildegard Foster-Heldmann, who heads the Danstadt cultural affairs committee, said that *"a comparison between Israel and Nazi Germany is absurd, disrespects the descendants of the Nazi victims and belittles the criminality of Nazi Germany."*

It was strangely fitting that an elderly New York Jewess had to go to Germany to be taught the difference between Hitler's Nazis and Israel.

She wrote an article entitled *"Zionist Israel's Final Solution for Gaza,"* a clear reference comparing Israel to the Nazis, on the *Intifada: Voice of Palestine* website.

Rosengarten signed a 2014 petition that appeared in the Huffington Post calling for *"the complete dismantling of Israel's apartheid regime, throughout historic Palestine – from the River to the Sea."*

Anti-Israel Jews are always greeted warmly around Europe. They are given celebrity and platforms on which to spout gruesome nonsense that is avidly lapped up by their audiences. Rosengarten's hate trip included stops in Berlin, Frankfurt, Bremen, Hanover, Heidelberg, Hagen and Gissen. Her schedule was eagerly advertised by the German-Arab Society.

In a troubling reply to *Jerusalem Post* questioning, the bank's spokesman, Dirk Hurtgen, said that he and his bank *"could not establish that anti-Semitic thoughts were expressed"* at the talk. When asked if he agreed with Rosengarten's statement that Israel is an apartheid state, instead of refuting this accusation he feebly said, *"I can't judge that."* Then he asked, *"Why is it relevant whether anti-Semitism took place?"*

As Efraim Zuroff, the head of the Jerusalem office of the Simon Wiesenthal Center, said, the role of the organizers involved in supporting Rosengarten *"reveals and ignorance of reality in the Middle East, and their reluctance to identify anti-Semitism paves the way for attacks on Israel that are groundless."*

He added that the people at Sparkasse Bank, with their history, *"should know better."*

Dr. Robert Neufroschel, the head of the Aachen Jewish Community which includes the town of Duren, said that Rosengarten's talk was a *disgrace, and of course anti-Semitic."*

You can see it wherever you look. It's in the media. It's in public statements by politicians and diplomats. It's on the campus, and it's chanted in street demonstrations.

Basically, it's nothing more than sly anti-Semitism.

Such events are taking place weekly throughout Europe where Jew-haters invite Jews to dump down on the Jewish state – and they call it anything but anti-Semitism.

THE DELUSIONAL STATE OF DENIAL.

They deny our existence. They deny our heritage. They deny out history, our belonging. They even deny the walls and shrines that scream our name.

It's not some state created in peace that they want. It is a delusional dream in which Israel doesn't exist.

It's not Filastin. It's Fantasy Land.

And we are expected to play along with this deception, to ignore our own rights. Dispense with our ownership. Throw away our property rights.

For what?

To accommodate these liars, these rogues?

What are we doing to ourselves?

We are indulging in the same fraudulent delusion as our enemy.

To what end?

To sleepwalk to our own oblivion?

This is nonsense. This is madness. This is fevered insanity to which no nation on earth has ever subscribed.

For Israel, a Palestine peace is an impossible hopeless partnership with a delusional vicious rogue state bent on our destruction.

It's time to call a spade the bloody shovel that it is.

As Yossi Beilin, the architect and driver of the Oslo process said after the ranting speech of Abbas, the leader of his disarrayed people, at the

United Nation General Assembly podium on September 30, 2015, *"I wish he would have called for the dismantlement of the Palestinian Authority."*

So ends the Oslo dream.

Abbas shattered the remnants of the illusion of Oslo. His authority was never a solution but always the heart of the problem.

This applies, with absolute certainty, to Hamas.

There you have the total failure of the Palestine project.

Israel acceded to international demands of allowing a Palestinian leadership to develop. They promised us the road map to peace. They gave us the path to our own destruction.

The Palestinian leadership, in all its ugly forms, have repeatedly said no to the creation of their own state, and yes to the deconstruction of ours. They impose on us the infamous four D's;

Demonization. Delegitimization, Denial. Death.

How much longer must we tolerate this delusional *"solution"* to the Israeli-Palestinian problem?

BDS. BUILDING A CAUSE AROUND A FRAUD.

BDS campaigns are not built on any solid foundation. They are built on a hypothesis, hypothesis being a proposed explanation based on limited evidence, or no evidence at all. It is used by BDS as their starting point and its lack of intellectual depth and honesty is draped in a mantle of emotional claims and sloganeering. No need to elaborate or produce facts or statistics. Emotional sloganeering is more effective in rousing support.

Something hypothetic is based on an imagined situation rather than fact. Everything in the BDS toolbox is based on hypothetical arguments devoid of facts. You know the list. Israel is an apartheid state when it isn't. Israel is conducting an intense blockage on Gaza when it isn't. Israel is conducting ethnic cleansing against the Palestinians when the condition and the population numbers of Palestinians have improved. Israel is a racist state when it is the most multifaceted nation in the Middle East and Africa.

They try to disguise the paucity of their argument in a form of tautology. They say and write the same simplistic things under different formats. They do this by attempting to recruit people in differing fields to declare their refusal to have any contact with their Israeli counterparts as if the message is being diffused globally but their statements are so shallow that they lapse into simplistic statements such as the one made by Professor Malcolm Levitt of Southampton University that made him look ridiculous.

In 2013 he said, *"Israel has a totally explicit policy of making life impossible for the non-Jewish population and I find it totally unacceptable."*

If, by Israel's non-Jewish population, Levitt is referring to Israel's Arab, Druze or Christians I challenge his foolish remark. These non-Jewish members of our community have it far better than their counterparts in much of the regions non-Jewish regimes.

In science and philosophy, Occam's Razor, is the principle of accepting the simplest satisfactory explanation. Atheists sometimes use the theory of Occam's Razor to prove that God is an unnecessary hypothesis in this physical world.

I would suggest that BDS is a perfect subject matter for Occam's Razor. They take two sides of an argument, their own and any Israeli claim. They then chip away any Israeli fact or evidence that disproves their contrary and pre-conceived view. They then present their biased hypothesis as if the other side has no challenging argument, leaving them to present the simplest explanation for perceived Israeli action, or non-action in a deceptive manner.

They take an alternative route to their own wrong conclusion by employing an illogical argument that proposes that, as the Palestinians seem weaker and poorer than the stronger and more prosperous Israel, the Palestinian condition must be a result of Israel oppressing and exploiting them. Known as a syllogism, a deductive conclusion reached by two or more assertive propositions, their assumption matches their desired aim, namely to point the finger of blame on to their intended target, the Jewish state. They can compound their conclusion by associating other false claims against Israel to their cause.

What is lacking in their inherently false assumption is the possibility of another piece of the syllogistic puzzle, namely that the Palestinian condition is based on their repeated rejection of generous Israeli peace offers that would surely have improved their lot.

This obvious hypothesis gets in the way of their prime obsession to blame Israel for all the ills of their tunnel-vision world. To accept this notion would expose the bankruptcy of their psychotic existence in which they have reveled on the high of bringing their ill-conceived views to a wider and receptive audience.

As such, BDS is an unnecessary and dishonest hypothesis.

WE ARE ANGRY.

We are angry at the incitement and the violence perpetrated by all factions of the Palestinians against us.

We are angry at the lies that we are destroying their mosques while they are burning down our Jewish holy shrines.

We are angry at the international condemnation of crimes we haven't committed, but are silent about the crimes that the Palestinians have.

We are angry at the slaughter of our people while the media fail to identify them as Jews in their obscene haste to highlight Palestinians killed without mentioning they were the ones executing the mayhem and murder.

We are angry at the BDS haters whose real aim is promoting the elimination of our country – a hate crime that goes unrecognized by a naïve or cynical world.

We are angry at all the United Nation's institutions that collaborate with the Palestinian plan to eliminate our country by hitting on Israel at every opportunity.

We are angry at European governments for their immoral voting record in United Nations forums that condemn Israel, and only Israel, for all the crimes and evils of the world. Abstaining from voting on such motions is immoral.

We are angry at the European Union who, even as we are being chased by knife-wielding Palestinian Arabs through our streets and homes, rewards their terror by shamefully introducing labeling sanctions on Jewish products - a discriminatory double standard they fail to apply to any other country.

We are angry that liberal democracies fail to stand with the only liberal democracy in a dangerous and deadly region.

Israelis are angry because we see a world that has learned nothing from their past, in fact they wish to repeat it, and that, at the end of the day, we Israelis can only depend on ourselves for our survival.

ISRAEL FIGHTING PALESTINIAN TERROR AND THE WESTERN MEDIA.

The old argument used to be that Palestinians were fighting and demonstrating to achieve a state of their own. The old argument used to be that it was Israeli obstinacy that fomenting Arab violence against Jews. The old argument used to be that Palestinian rage was caused by excessive Israeli military attacks against defenseless Palestinians. This was also known as *"disproportionate force."* Why wouldn't such a population rise up in anger when they are so *"oppressed"* and *"occupied,"* so the media said.

When I put pen to paper to expose the Jew hatred that lies at the heart of the Palestinian cause in my book *"Fighting Hamas, BDS and Anti-Semitism"* I did so to expose the facts and anecdotal evidence that the media tended to ignore.

The media preferred to point at Israeli policies, always using the language of "occupation" and "settlements," the language of left-wing editors. They made this the peg on which to justify Palestinian acts of violence against Israeli civilians. The twist of language permitted them to post obscenely inaccurate headlines.

Media headlines left the identity of the assailant anonymous as in *"Jerusalem bus and car attacks leaves dead and wounded,"* or *"Jerusalem attack kills three,"* or The Independent's headline that read as if Israelis were doing the attacking when, in fact, they were the victims of Palestinian Arabs attacks, *"'Israel attacks.' Guns, cars and knives are the new weapon of war in Jerusalem."*

Readers were left to guess who was doing the attacking and that Palestinian Arabs were the victims. None of the headlines explicitly mentioned that all the attacked victims were Israeli Jews.

So incensed was Lord Michael Grade, former chairman of the BBC Trust, that he wrote a letter of complaint slamming the BBC correspondent, Orla Guerin, for her misreporting of the ongoing violence carried out by Palestinians against Israelis. He was upset by her *"equivalence between Israeli victims of terrorism and Palestinians who have been killed by Israeli security forces in the act of carrying out terror attacks."*

He knew the facts. Other editors and bureau chiefs also knew but still posted biased headlines and editorial slants.

His letter follows an appalling BBC headline which read, *"Palestinian shot dead after Jerusalem attack claims two."*

BBC readers would never know that this described a Palestinian youth carrying out a terrorist attack that killed two Jewish men, seriously injured a woman and wounding her two year old son.

The overwhelming weight of three hundred plus pages of evidence in my book of the anti-Jewish tirades in support of an anti-Semitic Palestinian cause throughout Europe has never been adequately investigated by journalists. Nor have articles addressing this phenomenon been adequately allowed for publication in certain mainstream media outlets. Yet, even to lazy observers, the evidence is out there and readily available. It is so frequent and so public that is low-hanging fruit for idle journalists.

Despite the stark reality that the Palestinian cause was never about creating a new and peaceful state but rather about killing Jews and destroying the *"abomination"* of a Jewish state, a tiny island of progress in the midst of a radical and bloodthirsty Islamic region, the media remains rigidly in denial blindly holding to the mistaken notion that only by granting a volatile Palestine statehood will the area calm down and that the fault for this omission is solely Israel's.

It leads biased reporters, editors, and bureau chiefs to lie to their public.

The Reuters bureau chief, Luke Baker, falsely tweeted that undercover Israeli police threw stones at Israeli security forces and incited Palestinian youth to do the same. This story was repeated by AFP and EuroNews.

So frequent have these incidents of untruthful reporting been that a frustrated Prime Minister Netanyahu asked BBC's Lyse Doucet at a Jerusalem press conference, *"Are we living on the same planet?"*

When much of the Western media choke on identifying the victims of Palestinian violence as Israeli Jews you know there is a serious breach of trust at play that must be addressed.

Sadly, these headlines are commonplace as editorial discretion repeatedly tilts a bias that fails to allow truth and honest reporting to shine through.

A STERILIZED ANCIENT HATRED.

Tell me it's not about hating the Jew. Alas, all the evidence proves that this is what it is. An ancient hatred dressed up in the Palestinian cause. The evidence, the history, is overwhelming. They don't have to prove or deny it. They simply say *"Israel"* or *"Zionist"* instead of *"Jew."* The cause is sanitized. The cause is made sterile from criticism. Don't tell us we can't criticize Israel, goes their argument, but their Jew-hatred is exposed again and again and again in the Malmo Syndrome, in the Matisyahu Syndrome, in that café that allows Jews but not Israelis to enter, in academia that disallows both to have a voice that speaks for Israel.

THE UMBILICAL CORD OF PALESTINIAN LOVE AND ISRAEL HATRED.

Those that adopt the Palestinian cause use it as a club to beat Israel. Show me anyone who loves the Palestinians without hating Israel.

Their professed love of Palestinians is selective. They only love them if Israel is lurking there somewhere in their narrative.

They don't actively love them if Syria, Egypt, Jordan, Kuwait and other Palestinian abusers are in the picture. Then they go silent. I wonder why.

No BDS campaigns against Egypt for their blockade on Gaza. No pro-Palestinian protests outside Syrian embassies for their wholesale slaughter of Syrian-based Palestinians. BDS has nothing to say about Apartheid-Jordan that has kept Palestinian Arabs stateless, actually in refugee status, since 1948. No peep even against the Palestinian Authority that maintains refugee camps in the territories that they control and administer. How can you be a Palestinian refugee when you live under the control of the Palestinian Authority? Go figure, because I don't have the answer. Perhaps BDS does.

People who don't care enough about the fate of the Kurds, Yazidis or Druze, yell and scream about the Palestinian condition. Those who do nothing to help Tibetans overcome Chinese oppression, those who merely cluck about Rwanda, Sudan, and Darfur, suddenly discover the Palestinian cause.

If occupation is their shtick how they have no boycott campaigns against the hundreds of countries that have an occupation issues? How come it's only Israel that makes them mad?

This professed love for the Palestinians goes hand in hand with a professed hatred of Israel.

It is an exclusive hate that goes against all reason and logic, and it shows itself in the falsehoods, the perversion of facts, history and the blood libels that we Jews are so familiar after centuries of similar defamation.

BDS. THAT IRRITATING LITTLE FLY THAT WON'T GO AWAY.

BDS. It's that irritating little fly that you swat away on a hot summer's night.

You know what I mean.

It's there on the rim of your glass as you reach out for another sip of your chilled white wine, or the pest that's perched on that piece of sweet fruit that you want to taste.

BDS. It's an organism that festers on ineffectual faculties such as the American Anthropological Association - What have they ever done to progress mankind? The American Historical Association, known to some as the American Hysterical Association after their ridiculous denial of history and their boycott nonsense, neither they, nor BDS, impact beneficial faculties such as medical, scientific and chemistry research which represent the determined search for progress, and not BDS regressive politicking.

BDS. It's a disingenuous movement that claims to represent the interests of Palestinian Arabs as they deprive them of their self-respect by forcing them out of productive lives provided for them by a willing Israeli enterprise.

BDS. It's a failing entity trying to destroy Israel's economy even as the Jewish State prospers and thrives by its innovation and skills.

BDS. It's an irritating little fly on a hot summer's night.

THE BDS LIE OF PALESTINIAN DESPAIR.

BDS LIES when it says that Palestinian violence and terror are caused by *"the despair of occupation and oppression."*

If this were true why is it Muslim youth that carry out all the acts of Palestinian terror and violence and not Christian Arabs?

Are they not suffering from the same despair? Or does BDS imply that *"occupation and oppression"* is selectively aimed at Muslim Arabs only? It's absurd!

It's not about despair at all. It's about hope. It's about a promoted version of glory and heroism, and it's about corrupt leadership.

Palestinian violence and terrorism is integrally linked to the incitement and propaganda couched in Islamic terms that is fed to them by both rejectionist wings of the Palestinian leadership.

Like it or not, Hamas is the predominant force in Palestinian politics. Diplomats, the media and, of course, BDS prefer to downplay Hamas, converting them into representatives of the downtrodden people of Gaza suffering under an Israeli blockade but, in truth, Hamas represents the real face of Arab Jew hatred, the one that has ghosted over all the targeted attacks against Jews for a hundred years.

It shamelessly announces its ultimate goal publicly, it is enshrined in its evil Mein Kampf of a Charter that uses religious, political and even introduces humanitarian reasons why it is essential to kill Jews and destroy Israel.

It elevates the Islamic nature of Palestinian society to successfully bond the people in a higher spiritual aspiration to achieve its gruesome aims.

The corrupt Palestinian Authority has been robbing their people blind for decades. One only has to see the palaces of its leaders to see the blatant cronyism of its leaders. Arafat is reported to have stashed away over a billion dollars in overseas bank accounts.

According to Martin Indyk, the Clinton Administration Middle East negotiator, who knew Arafat intimately well, Arafat was always traveling the world, looking for handouts.

"Arafat for years would cry poor, saying, 'I can't pay the salaries, we're going to have a disaster, and the Palestinian economy is going to collapse.' At the same time he accumulated hundreds of millions of dollars."

Arafat used some of that money propping up rival terrorist groups each competing against the other to gain favor from their corrupt and patronizing leader.

Arafat was in word and deed the second Islamic arch-terrorist, the first being Haj Amin el-Husseini, the Grand Mufti of Jerusalem whose evil raison d'etre was the destruction of Jews.

In a real sense, Arafat followed closely in his footsteps. One of his many inspired terrorist outrages against Israeli civilians was called the Al-Aqsa Intifada which began in September 2000. Over a thousand Israelis were killed by Palestinian suicide bombings and shootings which resulted in an Israeli response and ultimately an Israeli distrust of Arafat as a peace partner.

Although assumed to have been a spontaneous reaction to the visit by Ariel Sharon to the Temple Mount, statements by people close to Arafat show that the Palestinian violence was premeditated by Arafat following his rejection of the generous peace offerings of Ehud Barak and Bill Clinton at Camp David.

Imad Faluji, the Palestinian Authority Communications Minister at the time, admitted months later that Arafat had planned the violence two months before the Sharon visit to the Jewish holy shrine as blowback over his failure at Camp David.

Ten years later, Mahmoud Zahar, one of the evil heads of Hamas, said that Arafat had instructed his organization to launch terror attacks following Camp David.

Even Arafat's widow, Suha, admitted, *"I met him in Paris after Camp David and he told me, 'You should remain in Paris.' I asked him why, and he said, 'I am going to start an intifada.'"*

What follows sounds eerily similar to what Mahmoud Abbas created in 2015.

Just prior to Rosh HaShana, the Jewish New Year, in the year 2000, the Palestinian Authority *'Voice of Palestine'* radio station began to put out calls *"to all Palestinians, come and defend the Al-Aqsa mosque."*

The PA closed all their schools and bused Palestinian students to the Old City and the Temple Mount to participate in organized "spontaneous" riots. When hundreds of Jews were praying below at the Western Wall, thousands of Arabs began hurling rocks and bricks at worshippers and police. The rioting spread to towns and villages throughout the West Bank and the Gaza Strip.

Arafat continued his incitement to violence. In January 2004, he called upon Palestinians to draw blood in an impassioned speech in which he whipped up the crowd by repeating the chant, *"With our souls and our blood, we will redeem you, Palestine. Until Jerusalem! Towards Jerusalem are marching millions of martyrs!"*

This speech was given after bus bombings in Jerusalem by his suicide bombers that killed forty Israelis and injured hundreds.

Not exactly the speech and actions of a peace maker. Talking to Western media in English, he called for *"peace of the brave."* For Israelis, he was calling for and giving *"peace of the grave."*

Not only has Mahmoud Abbas followed in Arafat's footsteps with his incitement to kill Jews, as with Arafat an incitement couched in Islamic terms, but other members of his administration have also used inflammatory language.

Jibril Rajoub, his sports minister, infamously said that if the Palestinian had a nuclear weapon they would nuke Israel.

Denis Ross, a former Palestinian-Israeli negotiator and an ardent two-state solution advocate criticized his own government for ignoring Palestinian incitement;

"The Palestinian systematic incitement in their media, an educational system that breeds hatred and the glorification of violence made Israelis feel that their real purpose was not peace."

But Rajoub and the Palestinian Authority is allowed to get away with their promotion of terrorism. They raise their future generations in the veneration of their terrorists by naming schools and sports events after killers of Jews, and the international community continues to pump funding into their educational system.

Incitement to genocide is an international crime. When propagated by an authority claiming statehood, as does the Palestinian leadership, this becomes state-sponsored incitement to genocide and terror. Why is the world tolerating this criminal behavior?

Generally speaking, incitement means encouraging others to commit an offense by way of communications such as broadcasts, publications or speeches.

Incitement to genocide needs to be proven to be direct, namely that both the inciter and the listener understand the implications of the call to action. There can be no doubt what the implications of Abbas's call to spill blood meant to the knife-wielding Arabs targeting Jews.

The fact that genocide did not occur is no defense in law for the inciter. Public incitement to genocide can be prosecuted even if genocide does not occur. A proof of result is not necessary for the crime to have been committed, only that it had the potential to spur genocidal violence. It is the intent of the speaker that matters, not the effectiveness of the speech that caused the criminal action.

Palestinian leaders such as Mahmoud Abbas and Ismail Haniya should be brought to trial for incitement to genocide. They cannot be considered in the international community as peace partners, but as criminals.

As such, they are the cause of the ongoing conflict. BDS hides this awful truth as they promote the lies of Palestinian despair. If there is any despair it derives from their corrupt leadership.

LET US MAKE THIS PERFECTLY CLEAR. RIGHT IS ON OUR SIDE.

No Jew set foot in any of the mosques on the Temple Mount. The only people that desecrated the Al-Aqsa mosque were the Arab rioters, the violent looters and pillagers who used the sanctuary as a fortress and arsenal for their violence, who brought in rocks and firebombs, who broke the furniture and doors to make barricades. They, the young Muslim men who call themselves Palestinians, they were the ones who defiled Islam's holy place with their dirty feet, not the Jews.

The only question remaining is did they do it against the will of the Wakf, the Islamic representative for the Temple Mount or Noble Sanctuary as it is known in the Islamic world, or against his objections? An investigation must be conducted to get at this important truth.

Their vandalism and violence was done with the blessing of Mahmoud Abbas and the world must know that Islam permits the desecration of one of their most holy places in the name of lies against the Jewish people.

The damage was done by Muslim youth with the will and approval of the Wakf, the Temple Mount imam. Therefore, the King of Jordan, who sees himself as the Guardian of this Muslim site, must condemn the Palestinian Authority and sack the Wakf for inciting and allowing this vandalism to take place and for damaging the name and holy sites of Islam.

Let me make it clear. The status quo was not changed or challenged on the Temple Mount during the Jewish high holy days of 2015 by Jews or Israel. Jews, Christians and others may have visited the site as they have done for decades but nobody disrespected the temples holy to Islam.

Israelis have nothing to apologize for. We were not responsible for what transpired recently on the Temple Mount, despite our strong claims to this most holy place. On the contrary, our security forces did their utmost to preserve law and order.

The sole cause of the violence and desecration were the Palestinian and Islamic leaders and the intense confrontation of the men and women recruited and paid for by the Islamic Movement in Israel. Known as the Mourabitoun and Mourabitat groups, they were bused to Jerusalem on a daily basis, not to pray but to perform acts of provocation on the Temple Mount and to create tension and violence there.

As any visitor can attest, they harass and insult any non-Muslims, particularly Jews. The Islamic organizations, supported by Hamas, the Palestinian Authority and external Muslim nations, attempt to challenge Israeli sovereignty of this site to the extent that they violate the safety of visitors and the security and sanctity of the site. As such, their exploitation of the holy site deliberately attempts to change the status quo.

After being banned from this place by their disrespect and disgraceful behavior they were allowed to take up strategic positions along the alleyways inside the Old City of Jerusalem that lead to the Temple Mount and the Western Wall, the most holy site in Judaism to insult, threaten, spit at, and assault Jews making their way to pray.

Against the background of this awful truth, they demand of Israel that we surrender this place to the will and control of the Palestinians for this is what they call part of *"east Jerusalem."*

They are demanding that Jews give up everything that justifies our rights for being there, that Jews must lend even more credibility to a Palestinian cause. What is incredible is that there are Jewish voices that support this notion. A culture of defeatism is being spread that allows the violent creep of Islam to take over what is ours. The message may be promoted in political terms but what we are experiencing is nothing less than the significant march of Islam in the Middle East, and the Jews of Israel are its last bastion.

Professor Ruth Wisse wrote about it two decades ago in her book *"If I Am Not for Myself: the Liberal Betrayal of the Jews."* In her work she described how the Arabs *"enlarged their war on Israel into an attack on the idea of Israel. Zionism, the Jewish claim to a land of their own, was declared racist because it deprived Palestinian Arabs of their homeland."*

The fact that Arabs never had a homeland called Palestine is irrelevant.

By skillfully inverting the facts of the Jewish national struggle, the Arabs substituted *"homeless Palestinian"* for stateless Jew. Arabs denied and blocked Jewish rights to their land. They blocked the Partition Plan that offered Palestinians a state. They made 850,000 Jews homeless and turned them into refugees. Yet, despite these awful facts, the Arabs and more recently BDS advocates try to convince a gullible world, including gullible Jews, that the Israeli and Zionist Jews are the guilty parties for building a successful nation.

There is a large consensus within Israel that agree that the Palestinian problem demands a fair, creative and humane solution, but the one-sided assaults against Israel and the denial of its legitimacy will achieve nothing. Gill Troy described this side in a Jerusalem Post article as, *"repudiating Jewish national rights while deifying Palestinian rights, and inflating this minor conflict into an international obsession, is unconscionable. Liberal critics exaggerate Israel's 'crimes' to justify championing a Palestinian political culture that is so vile. How else to explain vilifying imperfect but democratic Israel while romanticizing the sexist, homophobic, racists, violent, dictatorial, illiberal terrorists who declare themselves the 'sole, legitimate representatives of the Palestinian people.' claiming all of Israel."*

Troy went on to describe a far left distain for liberal Israel being stoked by some radical Jews whose anti-Zionism absolves Israel's enemies of their anti-Semitism.

"The cosmopolitan, anchorless 'non-Jewish Jew' has become the anti-Jewish Jew, attacking today's greatest Jewish collective project, Israel, nastily, globally, blindly, disloyally."

The Palestinians already have two states, one based in Gaza, the other based in Ramallah in what they call the West Bank but is more correctly known as Judea and Samaria.

The PLO is in power there - now. If the Israel Defense Forces withdrew from the Israeli controlled areas Hamas would certainly take over. We have seen this happen before. The PLO lost the Gaza Strip in a bloody civil war with Hamas. It will absolutely happen there. Should Israel withdrawal from territories we will see Hamas flags flying over Jerusalem.

The Arab Muslim has not come to terms with Israel's right to exist. It carries with it the pain of shame, a characteristic that has brought out the most negative traits in the Arab for centuries. Honor, it seems to an observer, is an Arab history of taking what is not theirs. Shame is the disgrace of not being able to achieve that goal. This is clearly reflected in the Arab struggle to defeat and destroy Israel.

In the current situation they attempt to rectify this fault by indoctrination and incitement, indoctrination that Jews have no history and, therefore, no right to be here, incitement that it is a holy Islamic cause to remove the Jews and destroy the Jewish state. Only by this, they say, can honor be restored.

This shame has been nurtured as a cultural psyche in the wider Arab world where those who call themselves Palestinians are kept stateless, often deprived of higher education and many jobs. They are raised with the sense that their honor will not be returned to them until they return to Palestine, a nation that never existed. Arab nations practice an absolute apartheid against Arabs claiming to be Palestinian, but you won't get to hear about it from the Palestinian cause supporters who fictionalize a narrative that demonizes and delegitimizes Israel but hides the truth about what is going on in countries that share the same ethnicity, language and religion of these stateless Arabs.

A new generation has been raised and educated in the hatred of Jews.

Despite this, one Middle East country in which Arabs have equal rights and the opportunity to live free and prosperous lives is Israel.

We have a moral responsibility to speak up and defend the State of Israel, the Jewish state. If we won't do it, who will?

We must speak up. We can never be silent. We own the title deeds to this place. These deeds derive from the Bible and enshrined in international law. And they are trying to deny us these rights.

I will not allow a false Palestinian voice define my identity.

Right is on our side! Justice is on our side!

WHY BDS CAN'T WIN.

In January, 2016, a group of emergency relief experts from Indonesia joined their counterparts from India and Sri Lanka in a six day disaster and emergency education seminar in Israel.

This was part of a major new initiative between the Jewish state and Múslim-majority states outside the Middle East.

Organized by Project Interchange – an educational institution within the American Jewish Committee – the guests visited several centers in Israel dealing with trauma, emergency management and medical rehabilitation.

Iswar Abidin, a disaster management consultant from Jakarta, revealed his reaction when he received the opportunity to visit Israel.

"It was very shocking, but I said to myself 'OK, let's do it!' I think it's something new and challenging."

For Trinimala Ningrum, the secretary-general of the Indonesia National Platform for Disaster Risk, all she had ever heard about Israel was war and terrorism. This was echoed by all of the mainly Muslim delegates who admitted they had to google Israel and Judaism to learn about the country they were about to visit.

Asian countries don't carry the baggage of anti-Semitism that most European countries have. Some of the participating countries are reaping the benefits of working with Israel in agricultural, water management, soil management and disaster relief projects.

The delegation's visit to the Barzilai Medical Center was an eye and heart opening experience. Dr. Hezi Levy, the Center's medical director, explained to them the issues of running a hospital under emergency conditions such as prolonged terrorist and rocket attacks and dealing with the four essential needs of a disaster situation – cooperation, coordination, leadership and training.

As she left the hospital, Ningrum explained that she had never heard the impact of the conflict from the Israeli side before.

The impact of gaining a different understanding of Israel was considerable for the participants. Until then, everything had been one sided.

Muhammad Ali Yusef, the Chairman of the Climate Change and Disaster Management Institution of the Nahdlatul Ulama, the largest independent Islamic organization in the world, said he hoped to organize an event in his own country where he could tell the Indonesian National Platform for Disaster Risk Reduction of their findings in Israel.

Victor Rembeth, the national manager of the Indonesian Disaster Resource Partnership, said, *"We Indonesians are blessed with your story and are going to tell it."*

In Rembeth's view, the benefit of the seminar showed *"how things can work"* with the program's *"people-to-people approach"* which has the potential to change the relationship between Israel and Indonesia.

There is a burgeoning connection between China and Israel. It is based on a Chinese appreciation and respect for the Jewish state.

When I visited China, people expressed their appreciation of China and Israel as being countries proud of their ancient and historic cultures. They told me they look on Israel as *"the Einstein Country."*

Their initial interest in Israel was academically focused. They were in awe of Israel's advancements in mathematics and science and were keen to discover what set Israel apart.

Chinese academics and entrepreneurs have no interest and little patience with the anti-Israel brainwashing and propaganda that has entrenched Western campuses. They find nothing in it that will advance China's march to the future. What they do find positive and attractive is Israel's accomplishments in essential fields of agriculture, medicine, science and technology-based industries and the commercial benefits to be derived from Israel's brilliance in innovation. It is Israel's ingenuity that attracts the Chinese and no amount of BDS nonsense will detract them from forging closer links with the Jewish state.

Little known is that Israel has the ability to communicate and do business with almost every Arab state. This is done discreetly. Impressive deals are signed that don't reach the pages of the daily newspapers. Occasionally, a news item is allowed to slip out. In late 2015, Israel opened an office in Abu Dhabi. This office in accredited to the International Renewable Energy Agency.

The recent change has been the willingness in the Arab world for informal, covert, ties with Israel. The breakdown in the world order, particularly in the Middle East, has caused Arab states to look for strength in collective security and they find Israel as a strong nation sharing many of their security and strategic concerns. This mutual interest translates into trade and technological cooperation.

The secrecy of the contacts make it difficult to gauge the size of commerce being transacted between Israel and regional Arab states, but there is little doubt that it is growing as rapidly as the recent discreet meetings between Israeli and Arab diplomats, security experts and businessmen.

Closer to home, and despite Israel's criticism of the European Union's double standards when it comes to conflict management, according to Carlos Moedas, the European commissioner for research, innovation and science, who also visited Israel in January 2016, Europe cannot do without Israel.

Speaking with Israel's President, Reuven Rivlin, he said, *"I love this country. I hope the cooperation between Israel and Europe will increase. For us, and for our scientists, it is extremely important. During my tenure I hope to be here for you, because you have been here for us in terms of everything in science and innovation."*

He went on, *"I want to be a little bit of your voice in terms of the great people I have met here and the many innovators and entrepreneurs. The drive and energy that you have in this country to create businesses is unique and is an example to Europe. I am here to tell you that I hope this cooperation will increase. Four us, and our scientists, it is extremely important."*

Israel has received 330 research grants with a value of up to three million Euros from the European Union. Two hundred of these grants went to the Hebrew University and the Weitzman Institute alone. To get this money you have to be uniquely good at what you do. As Carlos Moedas explained, the EU knows how to turn money into knowledge; it is less good at turning knowledge into money. This is where Israel excels. There were over one thousand five hundred new start-ups established in tiny Israel in 2015.

Moedas is the overseer of the EU's Horizon 2020, the world's largest public research program. Israel only came on board in 2014 and is already a prime component and contributor to this European research platform.

Israeli hi-tech exits generated more than nine billion dollars in 2015, according to the IVC Research Center.

This is one of the reasons why NASDAQ, the world's second largest stock exchange announced a joint venture with the Tel Aviv Stock Exchange (TASE) to build a private market for Israeli companies who are not yet 'ripe' enough to go public. This will greatly assist Israeli companies as they grow from start-ups to fully-fledged enterprises and IPOs.

If the aim of BDS was to ruin Israel economically, the nail in their coffin came with the official announcement that Israel's debt burden fell to below 65% in 2015.

The debt burden compares how much a country owes its creditors to the size of its economy. The debt burden drops when economic growth is larger than its budget deficit. Israel's deficit came out at 2.15% of GDP.

Israel's debt level is far below that of most advanced economies which average above the 100% debt-to-GDP level.

The improving strength of Israel's economy is bad news for BDS.

For all the money and effort they are putting into attacking Israel's economy with their boycott Israel campaigns, this is the clearest indication yet they are losing their strategic economic battle against Israel.

An added layer of protection for Israel against BDS is the US-Israel Trade and Commercial Enhancement Act. The United States Congress frowns on any form of commercial boycott. They go against the principle of free trade. This bill, which was introduced on October 10, 2015, discourages potential trade partners from engaging in economic discrimination by participating in or promoting acts of boycotts, divestments or even sanctions against Israel. Any country or company that attempts to impose BDS on Israeli goods or services and are benefiting from their trade with America by virtue of a free trade agreement may find themselves blocked and punished if they target Israel for discriminatory boycotting. As most of the countries in which BDS operates are those who value their trade with the US, this law will severely hamper BDS's efforts to injure Israel economically.

Truth be told, in the world at large they love our stuff and can't do without it.

BDS really is for idiots!

Made in the USA
San Bernardino, CA
27 November 2016